Published in 2021 by Welbeck Children's Books

An imprint of Welbeck Children's Limited, part of
Welbeck Publishing Group
20 Mortimer Street London W1T 3JW

ISBN 978 1 78312 713 9
Printed in Dubai
10 9 8 7 6 5 4 3 2 1

Author: Jon Richards
Text and design: Tall Tree Ltd.
Editorial Manager: Joff Brown
Design Manager: Sam James
Production: Melanie Robertson

FSC
www.fsc.org
MIX
Paper from
responsible sources
FSC® C004800

60-SECOND GENIUS

SCIENCE

BITE-SIZE FACTS TO MAKE LEARNING FUN AND FAST

JON RICHARDS

CONTENTS

CHAPTER 1

MATERIALS AND MATTER

CHAPTER 2

ENERGY

CHAPTER 3

FORCES

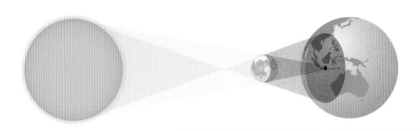

CHAPTER 4

SPACE

CHAPTER 5

PLANET EARTH

CHAPTER 6

LIVING WORLD

WHAT IS SCIENCE?

Scientists try to explain the world around us and why things happen the way they do. They do this by observing objects and events, and recording what happens and when. Scientists will then use this information, or data, to test different ideas (known as hypotheses) to see if they really work.

Even if the data supports an idea, things may change later. Advances in technology can reveal even more information that can change what we know completely!

Whatever happens, scientists will continue to observe events and record and collect information, helping us to improve our scientific understanding of the Universe and everything in it.

CHAPTER 1

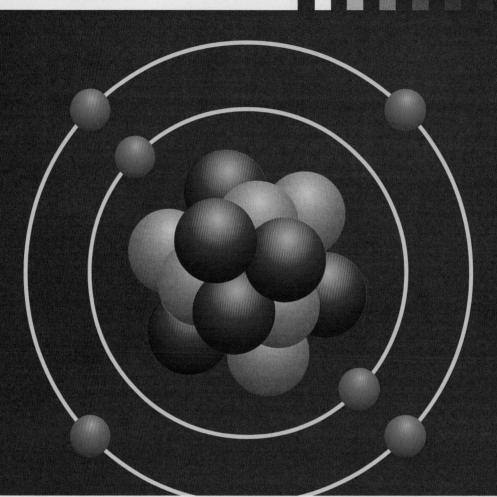

MATERIALS AND MATTER

STATES OF MATTER

Everything is made of matter—from the water flowing out of a tap to the clouds floating in the sky. Matter takes one of four different states, depending on the behavior of the tiny particles that make it up.

Solid
The particles in a solid are held together by rigid bonds. They cannot move about so the solid keeps the same shape and volume.

Liquid
The particles in a liquid can slide over each other. A liquid can flow freely, but it will keep the same volume. It takes the shape of any container it is poured into.

Gas
The particles in a gas can move about freely. A gas does not have a fixed shape or volume, and it will fill any container it is put into.

Plasma
This is a form of gas in which the particles have an electric charge. Stars like our Sun are made of plasma.

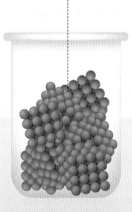
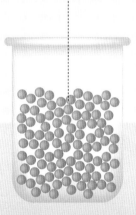

NOW TRY THIS!

Water is one of the few materials that exist on Earth as a solid (ice), liquid (water), and a gas (water vapor). Can you find examples of each state of matter around your home?

Plasma makes up more than 99 percent of the observable Universe. However, scientists believe that observable matter only makes up about 4 percent of the Universe. The rest is strange stuff we can't see, called dark matter and dark energy.

Matter changes from one state to another when the amount of energy in its particles is altered. If you reduce the energy, the particles move more slowly and may even stop. Increase the energy, and the particles move more quickly and may fly apart.

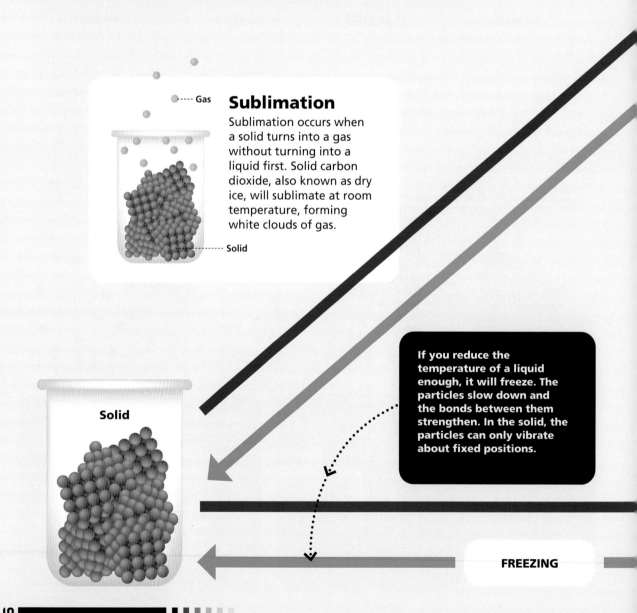

----- Gas

Sublimation

Sublimation occurs when a solid turns into a gas without turning into a liquid first. Solid carbon dioxide, also known as dry ice, will sublimate at room temperature, forming white clouds of gas.

------- Solid

Solid

If you reduce the temperature of a liquid enough, it will freeze. The particles slow down and the bonds between them strengthen. In the solid, the particles can only vibrate about fixed positions.

FREEZING

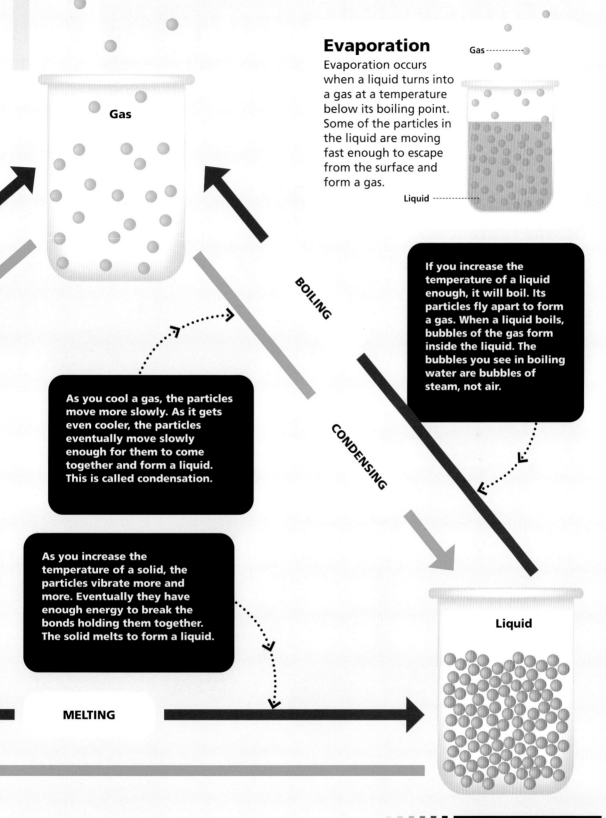

Gas

Evaporation

Evaporation occurs when a liquid turns into a gas at a temperature below its boiling point. Some of the particles in the liquid are moving fast enough to escape from the surface and form a gas.

Gas - - - - - - - -

Liquid - - - - - - - -

BOILING

If you increase the temperature of a liquid enough, it will boil. Its particles fly apart to form a gas. When a liquid boils, bubbles of the gas form inside the liquid. The bubbles you see in boiling water are bubbles of steam, not air.

As you cool a gas, the particles move more slowly. As it gets even cooler, the particles eventually move slowly enough for them to come together and form a liquid. This is called condensation.

CONDENSING

As you increase the temperature of a solid, the particles vibrate more and more. Eventually they have enough energy to break the bonds holding them together. The solid melts to form a liquid.

Liquid

MELTING

Most of the matter in the Universe is made up of atoms. They are too small to see even with powerful microscopes—millions could fit on the period at the end of this sentence. But even these tiny particles are made up of smaller subatomic particles.

Nucleus

At the center of an atom is the nucleus. This is made up of subatomic particles called neutrons and protons.

Neutron

Neutrons are found in the atom's nucleus. They have no electrical charge.

Proton

Electrons

These tiny subatomic particles have much less mass than neutrons and protons. They have a negative electrical charge. They whiz around the atom's nucleus in different layers, or shells.

Electron

Protons are found in the atom's nucleus. They have a positive electrical charge.

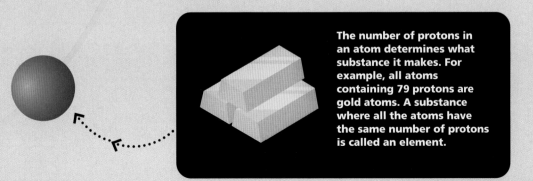

The number of protons and electrons in an atom are usually equal. Atoms may gain or lose electrons in chemical reactions, and plasma, as found in the Sun, consists of atoms which have had their electrons stripped from them.

Making molecules

Atoms aren't usually found on their own. Instead, they join with other atoms to form particles called molecules.

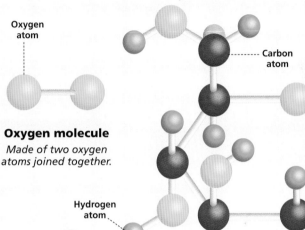

Oxygen atom

Carbon atom

Oxygen molecule
Made of two oxygen atoms joined together.

Hydrogen atom

Water molecule
Made of two hydrogen atoms joined to one oxygen atom.

Glucose molecule
Glucose is a form of sugar. Its molecules contain six carbon atoms, 12 hydrogen atoms, and six oxygen atoms.

The number of protons in an atom determines what substance it makes. For example, all atoms containing 79 protons are gold atoms. A substance where all the atoms have the same number of protons is called an element.

Scientists arrange elements in a grid called the Periodic Table. The elements are arranged according to their atomic number, which increases from left to right across each row.

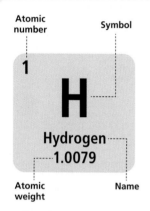

Atomic number

Symbol

1

H

Hydrogen

1.0079

Atomic weight

Name

Name and number

Each element is shown with its mass number and its atomic number. The atomic number refers to the number of protons in one atomic nucleus of that element. The mass number refers to the total number of protons and neutrons in each atomic nucleus.

What's in a name?

Each element is given its own symbol. This can be the initials of the element's name, such as C (carbon), or it can be a shortening of the element's Latin name, such as Pb (short for the Latin *plumbum*, meaning lead). Some elements are named after famous scientists. For example, copernicium (Cn) is named after the Renaissance scientist Nicolaus Copernicus.

The elements making up the block in the middle are called the transition metals. They include most of the common metals we see around us, such as iron, copper, silver, and gold.

1 **H** Hydrogen 1.0079							
3 **Li** Lithium 6.941	**4** **Be** Beryllium 9.01218						
11 **Na** Sodium 22.989768	**12** **Mg** Magnesium 24.305						
19 **K** Potassium 39.0983	**20** **Ca** Calcium 40.078	**21** **Sc** Scandium 44.95591	**22** **Ti** Titanium 47.88	**23** **V** Vanadium 50.9415	**24** **Cr** Chromium 51.9961	**25** **Mn** Manganese 54.938	**26** **Fe** Iron 55.847
37 **Rb** Rubidium 85.4678	**38** **Sr** Strontium 87.62	**39** **Y** Yttrium 88.90585	**40** **Zr** Zirconium 91.224	**41** **Nb** Niobium 92.90638	**42** **Mo** Molybdenum 95.94	**43** **Tc** Technetium 98.9072	**44** **Ru** Ruthenium 101.07
55 **Cs** Cesium 132.90543	**56** **Ba** Barium 137.327	57–71	**72** **Hf** Hafnium 178.49	**73** **Ta** Tantalum 180.9479	**74** **W** Tungsten 183.85	**75** **Re** Rhenium 186.207	**76** **Os** Osmium 190.23
87 **Fr** Francium 223.0197	**88** **Ra** Radium 226.0254	89–103	**104** **Rf** Rutherfordium (261)	**105** **Db** Dubnium (262)	**106** **Sg** Seaborgium (266)	**107** **Bh** Bohrium (264)	**108** **Hs** Hassium (269)

57 **La** Lanthanum 138.9055	**58** **Ce** Cerium 140.115	**59** **Pr** Praseodymium 140.90765	**60** **Nd** Neodymium 144.24	**61** **Pm** Promethium 144.9127	**62** **Sm** Samarium 150.36
89 **Ac** Actinium 227.0278	**90** **Th** Thorium 232.0381	**91** **Pa** Protactinium 231.03588	**92** **U** Uranium 238.0289	**93** **Np** Neptunium 237.0482	**94** **Pu** Plutonium 244.0642

The Periodic Table was developed in 1869 by the Russian chemist Dmitri Mendeleev.

Artificial elements

The elements that have an atomic number of 1 to 94 occur naturally on Earth. The 24 elements that have a higher atomic number have only been created artificially inside nuclear reactors, particle accelerators, or in powerful atomic explosions. These are known as synthetic elements, and for some of them only a handful of atoms have ever existed.

Groups of elements

The elements in a group (a vertical column in the table) all have some properties in common. For example, the Noble gases in the far right hand column are very unreactive (they do not form molecules or react with other elements). Scientists classify the elements into two main groups: metals and non-metals (see pages 22 and 23).

> The element carbon can combine with other elements to form nearly 10 million different compounds (substances whose molecules contain more than one element).

							2 He Helium 4.00260
5 B Boron 10.811	6 C Carbon 12.011	7 N Nitrogen 14.00674	8 O Oxygen 15.9994	9 F Fluorine 18.998403	10 Ne Neon 20.1797		
13 Al Aluminum 26.981539	14 Si Silicon 28.0855	15 P Phosphorus 30.973762	16 S Sulfur 32.066	17 Cl Chlorine 35.4527	18 Ar Argon 39.948		

27 Co Cobalt 58.9332	28 Ni Nickel 58.6934	29 Cu Copper 63.546	30 Zn Zinc 65.39	31 Ga Gallium 69.732	32 Ge Germanium 72.64	33 As Arsenic 74.92159	34 Se Selenium 78.96	35 Br Bromine 79.904	36 Kr Krypton 83.80
45 Rh Rhodium 102.9055	46 Pd Palladium 106.42	47 Ag Silver 107.8682	48 Cd Cadmium 112.411	49 In Indium 114.818	50 Sn Tin 118.71	51 Sb Antimony 121.760	52 Te Tellurium 127.6	53 I Iodine 126.90447	54 Xe Xenon 131.29
77 Ir Iridium 192.22	78 Pt Platinum 195.08	79 Au Gold 196.9665	80 Hg Mercury 200.59	81 Ti Thallium 204.3833	82 Pb Lead 207.2	83 Bi Bismuth 208.98037	84 Po Polonium (208.9824)	85 At Astatine 209.9871	86 Rn Radon 222.0176
109 Mt Meitnerium (268)	110 Ds Darmstadtium (269)	111 Rg Roentgentium (272)	112 Cn Copernicium (277)	113 Uut Ununtrium unknown	114 Uuq Ununquadium (289)	115 Uup Ununpentium unknown	116 Uuh Ununhexium (298)	117 Uus Ununseptium unknown	118 Uuo Ununoctium unknown

63 Eu Europium 151.9655	64 Gd Gadolinium 157.25	65 Tb Terbium 158.92534	66 Dy Dysprosium 162.50	67 Ho Holmium 164.93032	68 Er Erbium 167.26	69 Tm Thulium 168.93421	70 Yb Ytterbium 173.04	71 Lu Lutetium 174.967
95 Am Americium 243.0614	96 Cm Curium 247.0703	97 Bk Berkelium 247.0703	98 Cf Californium 251.0796	99 Es Einsteinium (254)	100 Fm Fermium 257.0951	101 Md Mendelevium 258.1	102 No Nobelium 259.1009	103 Lr Lawrencium (262)

A mixture is made from two or more materials that keep their separate features and identities without chemically joining or reacting with each other.

Types of mixture:

Coarse mixture

This mixture is made up of large sized particles, such as different stones on a pebbly beach mixing with sand and water, or even a mixture of nuts in a bowl.

Suspension

In a suspension, particles float about in a liquid, but they will gradually settle to the bottom over time, forming a base layer. Suspensions include particles of mud floating in water, which will eventually sink to the bottom.

Solution

In a solution, one substance, known as the solute, dissolves completely into a liquid, called the solvent. For example, salt crystals will dissolve and mix completely with water to form a saltwater solution.

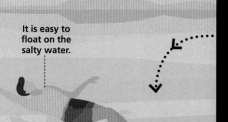

It is easy to float on the salty water.

The Dead Sea is one of the saltiest bodies of water on Earth. Its water contains nearly 10 times more salt than normal seawater. Scientists estimate that there are about 40.8 million tons (37 million metric tons) of salt in the Dead Sea!

Salt crystals form at the edges of the Dead Sea.

Mixtures can be split up quite easily if their particles are large or not mixed well. But mixtures that have small particles or are mixed completely, such as a solution, need more effort to split them.

Filtering

When a mixture passes through filter paper, the paper traps larger particles, allowing smaller ones, such as water molecules, to pass through. A face mask allows air particles to pass through, while blocking dust and smoke.

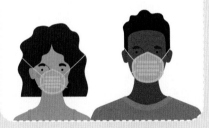

Boiling

Boiling a salt-water solution causes the water molecules to boil away, leaving the salt behind.

Centrifuge

A centrifuge spins a mixture around very quickly in a tube. The heavier particles are forced to the bottom of the tube, while the lighter ones stay at the top. For example, hospitals use a centrifuge to separate blood particles. Red blood cells are pushed to the bottom. Platelets and white blood cells are in the middle, while the plasma sits on top.

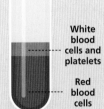

Plasma

White blood cells and platelets

Red blood cells

SEPARATED BLOOD

Chromatography

Mixtures such as ink are made up of substances with different-sized molecules. These can be separated by putting a drop of ink on paper. Water soaks up through the paper. The substances dissolve in water, and the ones with smaller particles travel farther through the paper than those with larger particles, spreading them along the paper strip. This method is called chromatography.

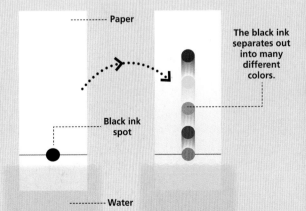

Paper

The black ink separates out into many different colors.

Black ink spot

Water

Distillation

Distillation is a method that involves boiling a solution made of two liquid substances. The gases from the boiling solution pass up a tube. The gas cools as it rises, and the substance with the higher boiling point condenses, turning back into a liquid. The other substance remains a gas and is cooled into a liquid later on.

REACTIONS

While some substances stay the same for long periods of time, others combine chemically, or react, with other substances, changing how they look and behave completely.

Inside a reaction

The substances involved in a reaction break apart into their individual atoms. The atoms then bond with atoms from the other substance, creating an entirely new substance that's made up of both chemicals. This is known as a compound. For example, **iron (Fe)** will combine with **sulfur (S)** to produce the compound **Iron Sulfide (FeS)**.

During a chemical reaction, none of the atoms are destroyed and no new atoms are created. The total mass of the substances reacting is the same as the total mass of the new compound.

IRON

+

SULFUR

=

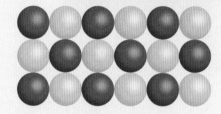

IRON SULFIDE

Speed of reactions

Some reactions happen slowly. **Iron (Fe)** combines with **oxygen (O)** in the air very slowly to form **iron oxide**, or rust.

Some reactions happen extremely quickly, resulting in an explosion. A violent explosion occurs when dynamite alters its chemical make-up.

Heated reactions

Burning, or combustion, is a type of reaction in which energy is released in the form of heat. This is known as an exothermic reaction. Burning requires three things: fuel, heat, and oxygen.

OXYGEN

COMBUSTION

FUEL

HEAT

Fossil fuels such as coal are also known as hydrocarbons, because they contain hydrogen and carbon. When they are burned in air, the hydrogen (H) atoms combine with oxygen (O) to form water vapor (H_2O), while the carbon (C) atoms combine with oxygen to form carbon dioxide (CO_2).

$$C + O_2 = CO_2 \qquad H + O_2 = H_2O$$

NOW TRY THIS!

Can you find examples of chemical reactions in your home? It could be gas burning on a stove to heat a pan, or an old bicycle rusting outside. Make a list of the reactions you find and see if you can identify the substances that are reacting, but take care when studying anything hot and ask an adult to help you!

ACIDS AND BASES

Liquids are sometimes classified by their acidity, which is a measure of how they react with other substances. The level of acidity is measured using a scale with acids at one end and bases at the other.

The pH scale

The acidity of a liquid is measured using the pH scale, which goes from 1 to 14, with 1 being very acidic, 7 being neutral, and 14 being a very strong base. Powerful acids and bases can be very harmful and can dissolve some materials, but milder forms are harmless—you can even eat and drink some of them.

Neutral substances sit in the middle and are neither an acid nor a base.

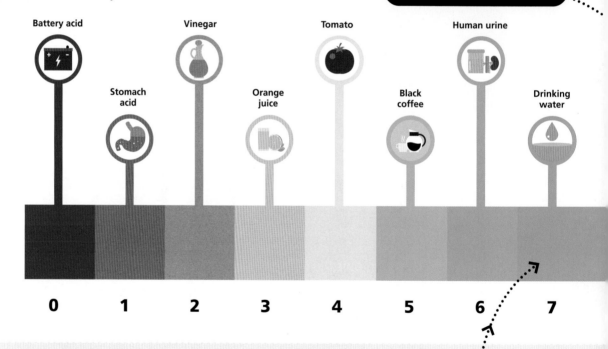

Battery acid

Stomach acid

Vinegar

Orange juice

Tomato

Black coffee

Human urine

Drinking water

0   1   2   3   4   5   6   7

Acids

Strong acids are very corrosive. They are used as powerful cleaners or in car batteries. One of the most powerful acids, hydrochloric acid, is found inside your stomach, where it helps to break down food. Citrus fruits and tomatoes contain weaker acids.

Milk has a pH value of about 6.5, making it a very mild acid.

Mixing acids and bases

Mixing together acids and bases produces an interesting reaction. They will cancel each other out to produce neutral water and a salt. They can also release gases. For example, if you mix vinegar (an acid) with baking soda (a base), this produces carbon dioxide gas which will bubble free of the mixture.

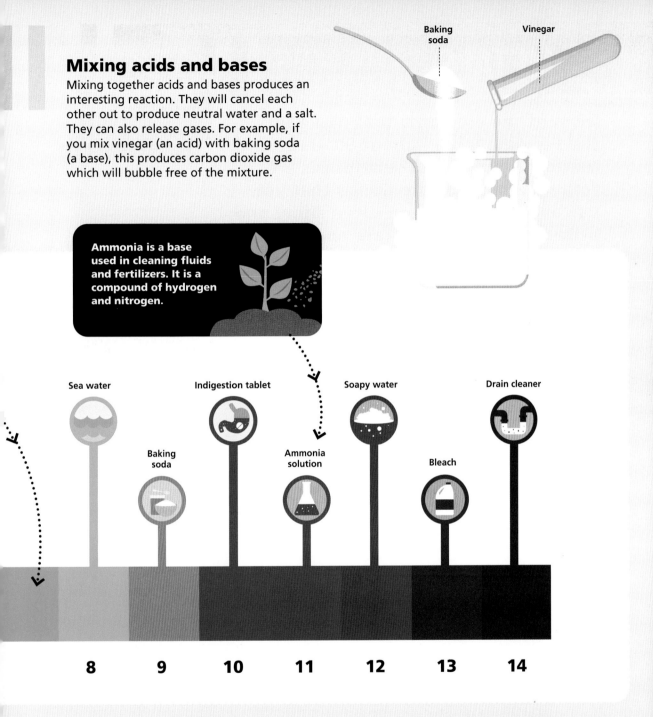

Baking soda

Vinegar

Ammonia is a base used in cleaning fluids and fertilizers. It is a compound of hydrogen and nitrogen.

Sea water

Baking soda

Indigestion tablet

Ammonia solution

Soapy water

Bleach

Drain cleaner

8   9   10   11   12   13   14

Bases

Strong bases include toilet cleaners, which have a pH value of around 14. If you have an upset stomach, you may take an antacid tablet, which is a weaker base with a pH value of about 10. A base that dissolves in water is called an alkali.

METALS

Most of the elements that make up the Periodic Table—about 90—are metals. These useful substances are found in many of the things that you use everyday. They are often shiny and attractive, and can be rare and valuable.

Metals

Periodic Table

The metals are mainly found on the left-hand side of the Periodic Table. They range from very reactive metals, such as Lithium and Sodium, to the much less reactive ones, such as gold and silver.

Properties of metals

Metals all have several properties in common. These are:

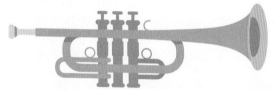

Shiny
They shine when cut or polished.

Conductors
They conduct electricity and heat well.

Malleable
They can be bent and shaped without breaking.

Most metals are also:

Solid
When at room temperature.

Tough and strong

High density

Sonorous
They produce a ringing sound when they are struck.

One metal that stands apart from the others is mercury. This shiny substance is a liquid at room temperature, and flows about freely. Mercury expands and contracts readily with changes in temperature, and was once used in thermometers. However, it is very toxic, and this use is being phased out.

Mercury ------

Platinum ring

Silver and gold coins

Gold watch

Precious metals

Some metals are so attractive that they are highly sought-after. These precious metals are hard to find in the ground, which has made them very valuable. They include gold, silver and platinum.

NON-METALS

The remaining elements on the Periodic Table are known as non-metals. Unlike metals, these substances are mostly dull, soft, and powdery, and they are not good at conducting heat or electricity.

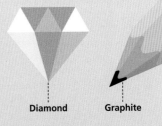

Non-metals

Most of the non-metals (such as oxygen) are gases at room temperature, one is a liquid (bromine), while the rest are solid at room temperature (such as carbon).

O_2

Properties of non-metals

Non-metals have several things in common with one another. They are:

Dull

Poor conductors
Of heat and electricity.

Easily broken
Making them weak and brittle.

Most non-metals are also:

Low density

Non-sonorous
Solid non-metals do not make a ringing sound when they are struck.

Carbon

This solid non-metal can exist in several different forms. One of these is graphite, which is a dark, opaque, and soft material often found in pencil leads. Another is diamond, which is an extremely hard and transparent material that is used to make jewelry.

Diamond   Graphite

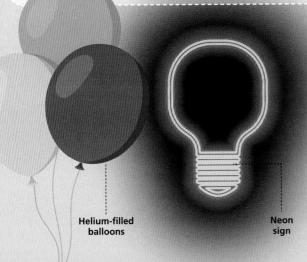

Noble gases

The elements in the column on the far right of the Periodic Table are known as the noble gases. Early scientists believed that these gases could not bond with other elements, so they were "better" or more "noble" than the other elements. They include helium, neon, argon, krypton, xenon, and radon.

Helium-filled
balloons

Neon
sign

HARDNESS

One way of classifying materials is to measure how hard they are. This is judged by seeing which other materials a substance can scratch.

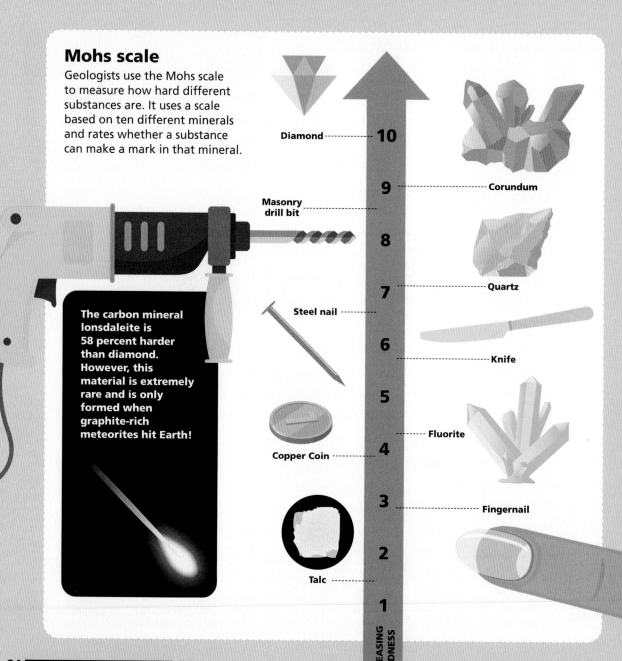

Mohs scale

Geologists use the Mohs scale to measure how hard different substances are. It uses a scale based on ten different minerals and rates whether a substance can make a mark in that mineral.

Diamond ---------- 10

9 ---------- Corundum

Masonry drill bit ---------- 8

7 ---------- Quartz

Steel nail ---------- 6

---------- Knife

5

---------- Fluorite

Copper Coin ---------- 4

3 ---------- Fingernail

2

Talc ---------- 1

INCREASING HARDNESS

The carbon mineral lonsdaleite is 58 percent harder than diamond. However, this material is extremely rare and is only formed when graphite-rich meteorites hit Earth!

While some materials are very hard and won't change under even the greatest forces, others can bend and twist without breaking. They can take on new shapes, or spring back to their original shape, ready to be bent and twisted again.

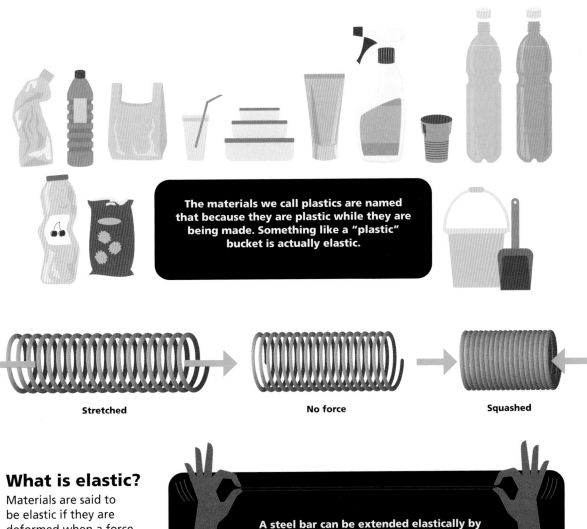

The materials we call plastics are named that because they are plastic while they are being made. Something like a "plastic" bucket is actually elastic.

Stretched   **No force**   **Squashed**

What is elastic?

Materials are said to be elastic if they are deformed when a force is applied but return to their original shape and structure when the force is removed.

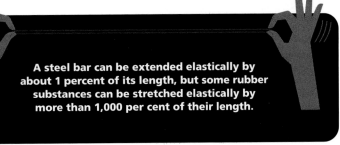

A steel bar can be extended elastically by about 1 percent of its length, but some rubber substances can be stretched elastically by more than 1,000 per cent of their length.

SYNTHETIC MATERIALS

Traditional cloth has been made from natural fibers, such as wool, for thousands of years. But in the last century, artificial materials from synthetic fibers have become available thanks to advances in chemical science.

The first synthetic fiber was nylon, which was first created in 1935.

Fleece jacket

Making fibers

To create synthetic fibers, two or more chemicals are mixed, creating a stringy mass, which is pushed through tiny holes called spinnerets. This produces long strands that can be twisted together to form the synthetic yarn. This is woven or knitted together to produce the material from which clothes are made.

Thermal vest

Swimming shorts

Cap

Training shoes

Strong and stretchy

Synthetic fibers are very strong and some are stretchy. This makes some of them ideal for making sports clothing, as they hug the body and help the athlete to move through the air or water, whether they are a cyclist or a swimmer.

Waterproof

Artificial fibers are very long-lasting and can be coated in waterproof chemicals that would damage natural fibers.

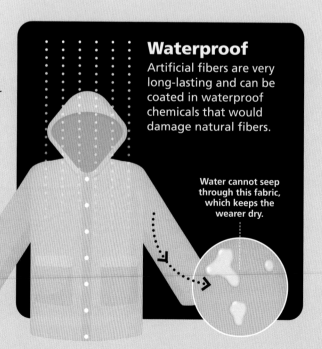

Water cannot seep through this fabric, which keeps the wearer dry.

COMPOSITES

Composite materials are made of two or more substances that combine to produce a tough, long-lasting new substance. Many machines and vehicles are made from the very latest composites, but the use of composite materials goes back thousands of years.

The Colosseum in Rome is a concrete amphitheatre.

Concrete

Concrete is one of the oldest composite materials. It is made from aggregate (usually sand or gravel), which is held together with cement and water. The ancient Egyptians used a simple form of concrete. The Romans were great users of concrete, and built the huge Colosseum in Rome, a concrete structure that is almost 2,000 years old.

Wattle and daub

This ancient composite material, dating back nearly 1,500 years, is made from a woven mesh of sticks (the wattle) covered in daub, which is usually mud or clay.

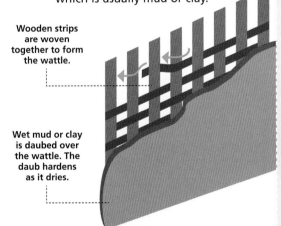

Wooden strips are woven together to form the wattle.

Wet mud or clay is daubed over the wattle. The daub hardens as it dries.

Fiberglass tennis racket

Fiberglass and carbon fiber

These modern materials are made from tiny strands of glass or carbon that are held inside a plastic. If the fibers are lined up in one way, this makes the material resilient to forces acting in that direction. Piling up many layers produces a super-strong material that can withstand powerful forces in any direction. Carbon fiber and fiberglass are lightweight and strong, making them ideal materials to make sports equipment, such as racing yachts and tennis rackets.

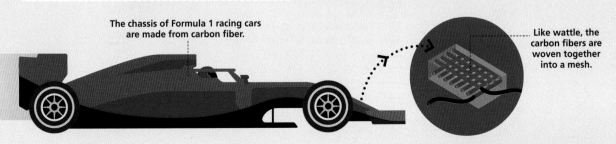
The chassis of Formula 1 racing cars are made from carbon fiber.

Like wattle, the carbon fibers are woven together into a mesh.

USING NATURAL RESOURCES

The Sun and Earth have supplied us with the materials and energy that we have used to build the towns and cities we live in and to feed more than 7 billion people. However, this supply is not limitless. If we continue to use these natural resources at the present rate, some of them will disappear very soon.

Farming

Fertile, well-watered land is essential for crops and farm animals to grow. However, bad farming practices and climate change can damage the soil, making it unfit for farming.

Every pound of beef that reaches the shops needs about 1,820 gallons of water to make.

Water

Water is essential in keeping us alive and to grow the plants and animals we eat. However, very little of the water on Earth is drinkable (see pages 92–93), and a lot of energy is needed to treat the water and make it safe to drink.

Minerals

Many of the things we use in our daily lives are made with minerals taken from the ground. These range from the bricks and rocks we use to construct buildings to the chemicals inside the electrical gadgets we carry around with us, such as mobile phones.

Renewable sources

Earth has plenty of energy resources that will not run out. These include the wind, waves, and sunlight. Harnessing these to produce electricity was expensive in the past. However, recent advances in technology have reduced these costs and will help to reduce harmful carbon emissions.

Recycling

Recycling objects and materials reduces the rate at which we get through natural resources. It also stops potentially polluting materials from getting into the environment.

Food waste

Plastics

Cards and paper

Glass

CHAPTER 2

ENERGY

WHAT IS ENERGY?

Energy is in action all the time as it makes things move, glow, feel warm, or change. It is stored inside objects, ready to be released when the time is right.

Stored forms of energy

Energy can be stored in an object in many ways:

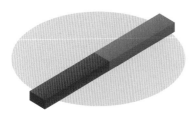

Magnetic

Magnetic energy is stored when attracting poles are pulled apart or when repelling poles are pushed together.

Chemical

The energy holding atoms together in molecules.

Internal (thermal)

The total energy within substances, usually caused by the vibrations of its particles. In cold objects, the particles vibrate slowly, while in hot objects the particles vibrate quickly.

Kinetic

The energy stored in a moving object.

Nuclear

The energy stored inside an atom's nucleus.

Electrostatic

Energy stored when attracting charges are pulled apart or when repelling charges are pushed together.

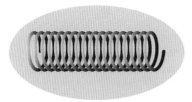

Elastic potential

Energy stored when an elastic object is pulled or pushed out of shape.

Gravitational potential

Energy stored when an object is raised up.

Inside every object and substance, the particles vibrate (in a solid) or move around (in a liquid or gas). This is heat energy. The more the particles vibrate, the more heat energy the object or substance has, whether it's an ice cube in a cool drink or the extreme heat in the core of a star.

Measuring heat

Temperature is a measure of how quickly the particles that make up an object vibrate, or how much kinetic energy they have. Temperature is measured in degrees Fahrenheit (°F) or Celsius (°C). This is the average kinetic energy of all of the particles in an object.

Absolute zero is the lowest possible temperature. At this point, all the particles that make up matter stop moving, which means that there is no heat energy. It occurs at

-459.67°F.

Feel the heat

Above absolute zero, particles behave in different ways, and they can change state depending on their structure and their temperature (see pages 10–11). At super-high temperatures, atoms can break down altogether, producing strange subatomic particles. The highest temperature ever measured is 7.2 trillion°F or 4 trillion°C (that's a 4 followed by 12 zeroes!). It was recorded in the atom smasher at the Brookhaven National Laboratory, New York, USA.

Transferring heat

Heat can move around from place to place and from one object to another by one of three ways.

Conduction The heat energy is transferred from one particle to another when they come into contact with each other. Heat energy is conducted from hot areas to cooler areas, such as from the pan to its handle.

Convection This occurs in fluids (gases and liquids). Part of the fluid is heated and becomes less dense than the fluid around it, so it rises. As it rises it cools, spreads out, and eventually sinks again, before being heated again to form a circular current.

Radiation This way does not require particles to transfer their energy. Instead, energy moves via invisible forms of radiation, such as infrared (see pages 40–41). Energy from the Sun travels through the vacuum of space as radiation.

NUCLEAR ENERGY

Atoms may be tiny, but they contain huge amounts of energy. This energy can send electricity to our homes and even power the heart of a blazing star.

Nuclear decay

Some atoms are unstable and break up, or decay, over time. When they break up, they release radioactivity in the form of tiny bits of atoms (alpha particles), electrons (beta particles), or waves of energy (gamma rays).

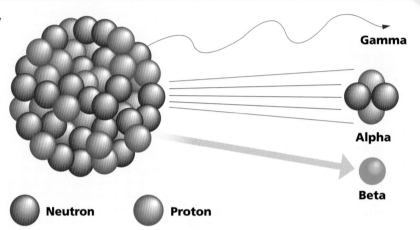

Gamma

Alpha

Beta

Neutron   **Proton**

Nuclear fission

Fission

The nuclei of atoms are held together by huge amounts of energy. Splitting these nuclei apart releases this energy in a process called nuclear fission. Tiny neutrons are fired at the nucleus of a large atom, such as uranium, causing it to split apart, releasing energy and more neutrons. This process carries on in a chain reaction.

Nuclear fusion

Fusion

Deep in the heart of the Sun, huge pressure and temperatures squeeze together atomic nuclei, causing them to form bigger nuclei. This is called nuclear fusion, and it releases the huge amounts of energy that we experience as light and heat.

Nuclear power station

A nuclear power station uses the energy released by nuclear fission to heat water, turning it into steam to turn a generator and produce electricity.

MAKING WAVES

Energy travels from one place to another in the form of waves. Examples of waves include a ripple spreading out on a pond and light traveling through space.

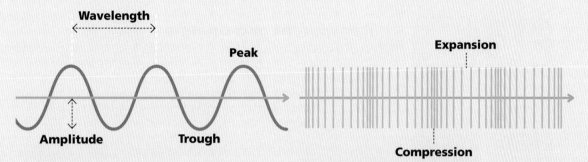

Transverse waves

These are waves that vibrate at right angles to the path the energy is moving in. The waves form peaks and troughs as they move.

Longitudinal waves

These are waves that vibrate in the same direction as the path the energy is moving. They form compressed areas and stretched-out areas, like the peaks and troughs of transverse waves.

Shaking the ground

Earthquakes are caused by a sudden movement in the pieces that make up Earth's outer crust. The energy they release travels through the ground as both transverse and longitudinal waves.

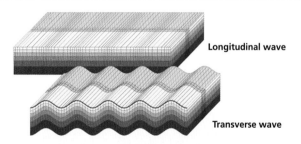

Longitudinal wave

Transverse wave

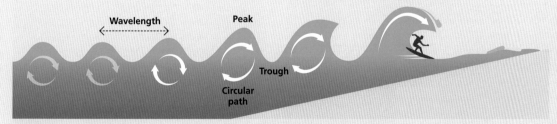

Water waves

The energy released by throwing a stone into a pool or by wind blowing over the surface of water produces waves that spread out from the disturbance. The water particles themselves do not move along with the wave. Instead, they move in a circular path, producing a moving wave of energy.

Look around you now and you will see light in action. Light allows you to see things in lots of colors, and from bright shining objects to dim and dark areas.

Transparent and opaque

Some materials, such as clear glass, let light pass through them without affecting it. These materials are called transparent. Other substances do not let light pass through them. Instead, they absorb or reflect all the light. These materials are called opaque. Materials that only let some light through are called translucent.

In the dark

When light is blocked by an opaque object, it produces a dark area called a shadow. The area at the middle of the shadow is called the umbra and it is usually completely dark. Around the edges of the umbra is a lighter area called the penumbra.

The umbra is the darkest part of the shadow, where no light from the source reaches the surface.

The penumbra is a fainter shadow where some light from the source can reach the surface.

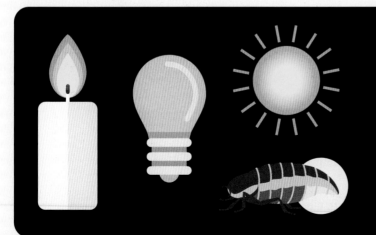

Light sources

Objects that produce light are called light sources and they produce light in different ways. A light bulb uses electricity to produce light, while a candle burns wax. The Sun's light is created by nuclear reactions, while some animals, such as fireflies, make light by mixing chemicals inside their bodies.

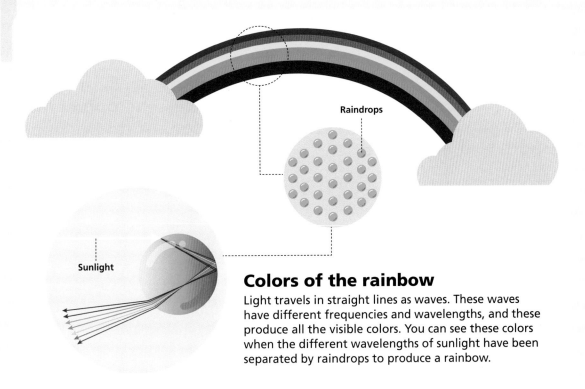

Raindrops

Sunlight

Colors of the rainbow

Light travels in straight lines as waves. These waves have different frequencies and wavelengths, and these produce all the visible colors. You can see these colors when the different wavelengths of sunlight have been separated by raindrops to produce a rainbow.

Detecting light

You detect light using your eyes. Rays of light pass into your eye and hit a sensitive area at the back called the retina. This is covered with special cells, which send signals to your brain when light hits them. Your brain interprets these signals to form a picture of the world around you. The image on the retina is upside-down! Luckily, your brain turns it back the right way up.

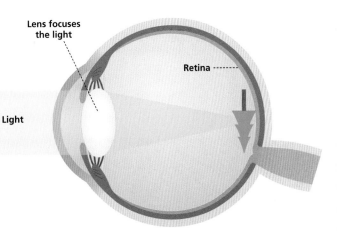

Lens focuses the light

Retina

Light

Light moves very quickly, at a speed of
186,282 miles per second
and takes a little more than 8 minutes to travel the
93 million miles from the Sun to Earth.

REFLECTION AND REFRACTION

While light travels in straight lines, its path can be affected when it comes across an object or material. The object may bounce the light away in another direction, or it may bend its path and produce distorted images.

Bouncing

Shiny surfaces, such as a metal or a mirror, will cause light to bounce away, or reflect. A light ray that hits the mirror is called the incident ray, while the ray that is bounced away is called the reflected ray. The angle that the incident ray hits the mirror is called the angle of incidence and, on a flat mirror, it is equal to the angle of reflection.

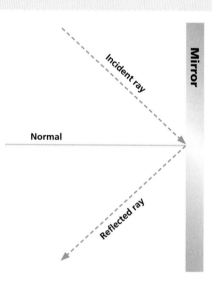

Incident ray

Mirror

Normal

Reflected ray

Making an image

As the reflected light rays bounce off the mirror, they produce a virtual image that appears to be behind the mirror. On a flat mirror, the distance the image appears to be behind the mirror is equal to the distance the object is from the mirror.

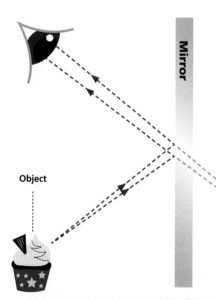

Mirror

Object

Image appears to be the same distance behind the mirror.

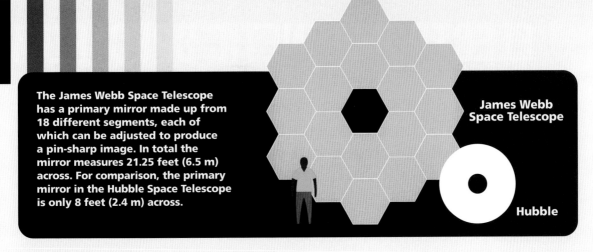

The James Webb Space Telescope has a primary mirror made up from 18 different segments, each of which can be adjusted to produce a pin-sharp image. In total the mirror measures 21.25 feet (6.5 m) across. For comparison, the primary mirror in the Hubble Space Telescope is only 8 feet (2.4 m) across.

James Webb Space Telescope

Hubble

Bending light

As rays of light pass through one substance to another, for instance, when passing from air though glass, they are bent, or refracted. You can see this when looking at a pencil standing in a glass of water. The pencil appears bent as the rays of light have to travel through water, glass, and air before reaching your eyes.

Concave

Magnifying rays

If you shape pieces of glass, you can bend light rays in different ways to produce enlarged and focused images. Convex lenses (with the sides bending outward) will bend light rays together. They are found in magnifying glasses and binoculars. Concave lenses (with the sides bending inward) will make light rays spread apart. These lenses are used in some spectacles.

Convex

Bending light with gravity

Black holes have such a powerful force of gravity that they can bend light traveling from objects that are behind them. This is called gravitational lensing and it produces a distorted image or even multiple images of the distant object.

Image of distant object

Black hole

Distant object

Image of distant object

ELECTROMAGNETIC SPECTRUM

The light you can see forms a small part of a range of waves called the electromagnetic spectrum. You cannot see most of this spectrum, but you will have come across objects that use its invisible forms.

The whole spectrum

The wavelength of energy changes as you move along the electromagnetic spectrum, from long-wavelength radio waves to very short-wavelength gamma rays.

Mobile phone mast

TV remote control

Radio telescope

FM radio and TV

Radio waves
These have wavelengths that measure from a few fractions of an inch to hundreds of thousands of miles. Astronomers detect radio waves from distant objects using radio telescopes, while we use radio waves to send signals that can travel right around the planet.

Microwaves
We use microwaves to heat food and to carry mobile phone signals from our phones to nearby communication towers.

Infrared rays
Warmer objects give off infrared rays. TV remote controls also use infrared rays.

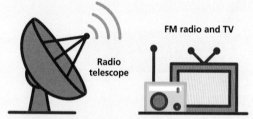

Radio waves   Microwaves   Infrared

Wavelengths at this end of the electromagnetic spectrum are very long and can measure nearly
62,000 miles.

Visible light
This is the part of the electromagnetic spectrum that humans can see.

Many mobile phone cameras can see invisible infrared light. If you view a TV remote control through a mobile phone camera screen, you will be able to see the infrared light blinking when you press a button.

Sun

X-ray machine

Radioactive elements

Ultraviolet light
The Sun produces ultraviolet light. This form of energy can damage skin cells, which can be protected from its harmful effects by covering up or using sunscreen.

X-rays
These waves can pass through the soft parts of your body, but are absorbed or reflected by the hard parts, such as your teeth and bones. X-rays are used to make images of the insides of your body, to check for broken bones and other problems.

Gamma rays
This high-energy part of the electromagnetic spectrum is produced by very hot and very active objects, such as pulsars and black holes.

Ultraviolet

X-rays

Gamma rays

Wavelengths at this end of the electromagnetic spectrum are very short and can measure

one trillionth of a metre
(one picometre).

SOUND

Whether it's music from a radio or the rumble of a bus, sounds come in a range of forms. Sounds are longitudinal waves that can travel through solids, liquids, and gases and into your ears, where they are turned into signals that are sent to the brain.

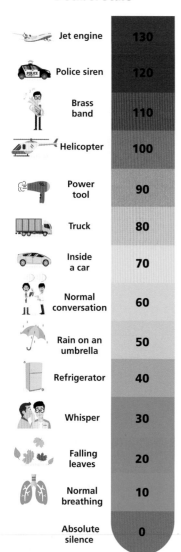

Decibel scale

Jet engine	130	
Police siren	120	
Brass band	110	
Helicopter	100	
Power tool	90	
Truck	80	
Inside a car	70	
Normal conversation	60	
Rain on an umbrella	50	
Refrigerator	40	
Whisper	30	
Falling leaves	20	
Normal breathing	10	
Absolute silence	0	

Volume

The volume of a sound, also known as its amplitude, is how loud or quiet the sound is. On a wave diagram, it is shown by the height a peak (or depth of a trough). The taller the peak, the louder the sound.

Getting louder

The volume of a sound is measured using units called decibels.

The explosion of the volcano Krakatoa, Indonesia, in 1883 was the loudest sound ever detected. It was heard more than 2,800 miles (4,500 km) away right across the Indian Ocean.

Double bass has a low pitch.

Violin has a high pitch.

Pitch

A sound's pitch is a measure of how high or low it is. The pitch is determined by the frequency of the sound, or how many times it vibrates each second. Sounds with a high frequency have a high pitch, while those with a low frequency have a low pitch. The frequency of sound is measured using units called hertz (Hz).

Speed of sound

Sounds move by passing the energy of their vibration from one molecule to the next. They cannot travel through a vacuum, and they travel faster through solids and slowest through gases.

The speed of sound through air at sea level is
1,125 ft/s,
while in water, it is
4,859 ft/s
and in diamond, it is
39,370 ft/s.

Quality

The quality of a sound, or its timbre, is what makes one tone sound different from another. This is why a bell will sound very different from a violin, and a cat will sound very different from a train.

Seeing with sound

Some animals use sound to detect objects around them. Dolphins and bats produce ultrasonic sound waves (sounds that are too high-pitched for humans to hear), which bounce off prey as echoes. They listen out for these echoes and are able to calculate where the prey is as well as how quickly it is moving and in what direction.

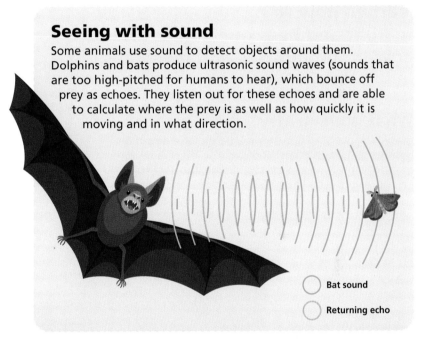

○ Bat sound

○ Returning echo

Range of hearing

Humans are able to hear a wide range of sounds, from low- to high-pitched. But some animals have hearing ranges even greater than ours, detecting sounds that are much lower- or higher-pitched than we can hear.

Range (in Hz):

0	40,000	75,000	100,000	150,000

Human 64–23,000

Dog 67–45,000

Elephant 16–12,000

Porpoise 75–150,000

Bat 2,000–110,000

The flash of a bolt of lightning and the glowing light bulb are both powered by electricity. While a powerful bolt of lightning can have devastating effects, we have learned how to harness electricity to light and heat our homes and to power our vehicles and machines.

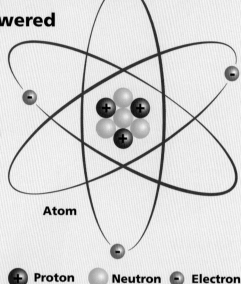

Atom

What is electricity?

Everything is made from atoms, and the atoms contain positive charges (protons) and negative charges (electrons). Electricity is the movement of a charge, usually negative electrons, or the build-up of these charges in one place.

+ **Proton**   ● **Neutron**   - **Electron**

Lightning flash

Static electricity and lightning

Static electricity is created when an electric charge builds up in one place. The movement and rubbing together of ice particles in a storm cloud can build up an electric charge. If this charge becomes big enough, it is released as lightning.

A bolt of lightning has up to

5 billion joules of energy

—enough to power a house for a month.

Create static electricity by rubbing a balloon against your sweater to build up a static charge in the balloon. Hold the balloon against your hair and you'll notice that the charge in the balloon creates an opposite charge in your hairs causing them to stand on end.

Conductors and insulators

Rubber insulation **Copper wire**

Some materials, such as metals, allow electricity to flow through them easily. These materials are known as conductors, and they are used to make the parts in electrical goods and gadgets. Other materials, such as plastic, stop electricity from flowing through them. These are known as insulators, and they are used to cover electrical wires.

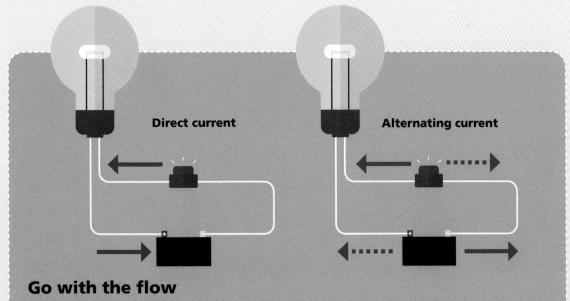

Direct current

Alternating current

Go with the flow

Current electricity involves the movement of electrons. In order to flow, current electricity needs a complete ring, or circuit, of a conducting material. The electricity can flow along this circuit in one of two ways. It can either move in one direction, known as direct current (DC), or the electrons can move back and forth many times a second, known as alternating current (AC).

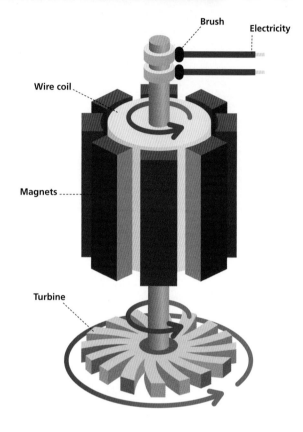

Brush

Electricity

Wire coil

Magnets

Turbine

Electricity is a convenient way to power the gadgets and machines that fill our homes and factories. It is made using various energy sources at power stations.

Generators

Electricity is usually made using large machines called generators. Large wire coils spin inside a magnetic field, and this spinning generates an electric current. To keep the coils spinning, air, steam, or water is pushed through a bladed wheel, called a turbine.

Coal

Oil

Gas

Fossil fuels

Burning fossil fuels, such as oil, coal, and gas, releases large amounts of energy as heat. This heat is used to boil water, turning it into steam, which sets the turbine spinning. Burning fossil fuels releases lots of carbon dioxide, which is contributing to climate change.

Solar power

We can harness the Sun's power to produce electricity in two ways. Photovoltaic (PV) cells convert sunlight directly into electricity. Concentrated solar power focuses sunlight using lenses or mirrors to heat water or other liquids to turn turbines.

Earth receives more energy from the Sun in a single hour than humans use in an entire year.

Wind power

Large wind turbines, some with blades measuring more 164 feet (50 m) long, are set spinning by the wind. Many of these large wind turbines are located out at sea.

Nuclear power

Inside the center, or core, of a nuclear reactor, nuclear fission reactions (see page 34) produce the heat that turns water into steam to drive the turbines.

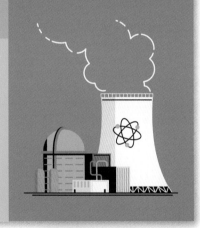

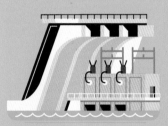

Hydroelectricity

Hydroelectric power is produced by harnessing the flowing movement of water. This may be the constant movement of a river, the sudden release of water from a reservoir through a turbine system, or the daily back and forth movement of the tides.

Storing electricity

Batteries store energy so that it can be used later. They store the energy in chemicals. The energy is released when the chemicals react with each other, creating electricity.

One of the world's largest batteries has been built in California, USA. The 250 MW Gateway project can produce enough electricity to power

150,000 homes
for one hour.

ENERGY RESOURCES

With more than 7.5 billion people on the planet, demand for power is huge, creating a growing need to increase electricity production. We also need to reduce the damaging environmental effects created by the more polluting ways to generate electricity.

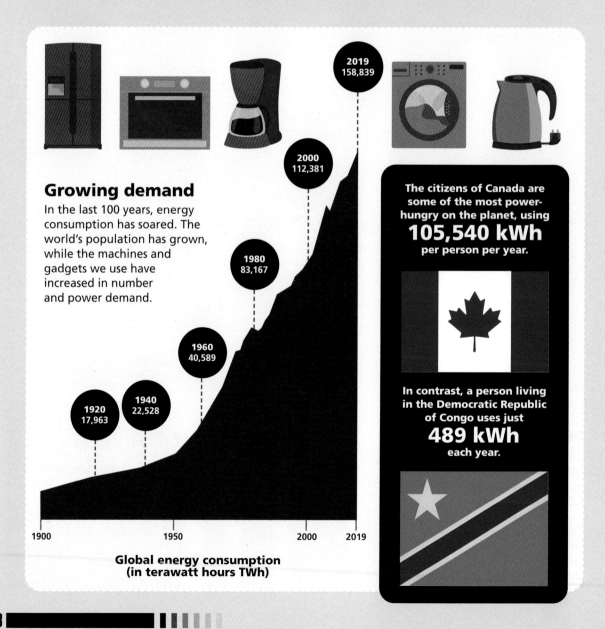

2019
158,839

2000
112,381

Growing demand
In the last 100 years, energy consumption has soared. The world's population has grown, while the machines and gadgets we use have increased in number and power demand.

1980
83,167

1960
40,589

1920
17,963

1940
22,528

1900   1950   2000   2019

**Global energy consumption
(in terawatt hours TWh)**

The citizens of Canada are some of the most power-hungry on the planet, using

105,540 kWh
per person per year.

In contrast, a person living in the Democratic Republic of Congo uses just

489 kWh
each year.

Primary energy demand

At present, fossil fuels still account for 80% of global energy demand.

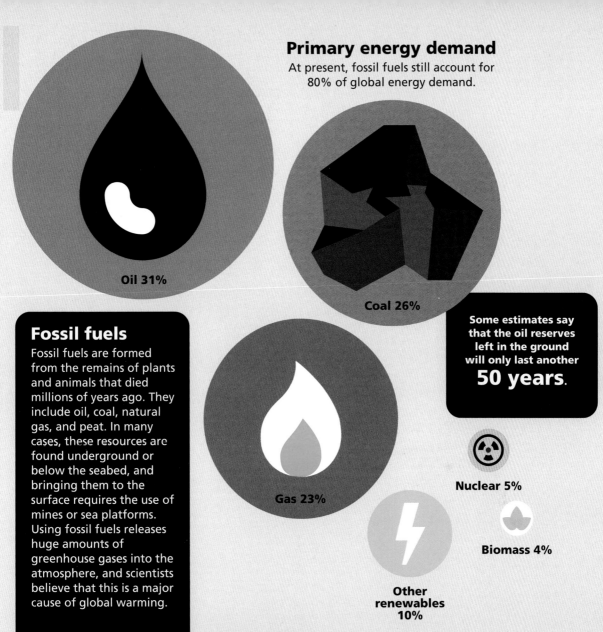

Oil 31%

Coal 26%

Gas 23%

Some estimates say that the oil reserves left in the ground will only last another **50 years**.

Nuclear 5%

Biomass 4%

Other renewables 10%

Fossil fuels

Fossil fuels are formed from the remains of plants and animals that died millions of years ago. They include oil, coal, natural gas, and peat. In many cases, these resources are found underground or below the seabed, and bringing them to the surface requires the use of mines or sea platforms. Using fossil fuels releases huge amounts of greenhouse gases into the atmosphere, and scientists believe that this is a major cause of global warming.

Micro power generating

Many homes and office buildings around the world are fitted with solar panels and small wind turbines to generate electricity on a small scale. Ground source heat pumps take heat energy from below the ground to heat the inside of the house.

CHAPTER 3

FORCES

WHAT ARE FORCES?

Forces are pushes or pulls that act on an object in a particular direction. They can make the object's movement faster or slower, change the object's shape, or even destroy it altogether. You might not be able to see a force, but you can see and feel the effects of many kinds of forces all around you.

Forces around you

Forces in atoms

Inside every atom powerful forces hold its nucleus together. These forces are released in the explosion of an atomic bomb or inside the reactor of a nuclear power station.

Gravity and weight

You feel the force of gravity on you all the time. It pulls you down to the ground, resulting in your weight.

Electromagnetism

This force affects all electrically charged particles. It controls electricity, magnetism, and light. Electromagnetism acts on particles to either attract them or push them away (repel them).

Forces are measured using units called newtons, with the symbol N.

When one force pushes on an object, another force pushes back in the opposite direction. Often, many forces are acting on an object at the same time. These forces can combine with each other to increase the effect, or they may act against one another.

Balanced forces

When two equal forces act against each other in opposite directions, they cancel each other out. These are described as balanced forces. When this happens, an object that was standing still remains that way, while an object that was moving continues to move at the same speed and in the same direction. Books on a table are pulled by gravity, but the table pushes back with equal force.

Unbalanced forces

When forces acting against each other are not equal, the forces are unbalanced. The difference between the two forces is called the resultant force. An object that was standing still will start to move in the direction of the resultant force, while an object that was already moving will change its speed or direction. To move forward on a bicycle, you need enough force to overcome the forces (friction and air resistance) acting against the direction you want to travel.

Newton's Laws

The British scientist Sir Isaac Newton (1643–1727) developed these three Laws of Motion.

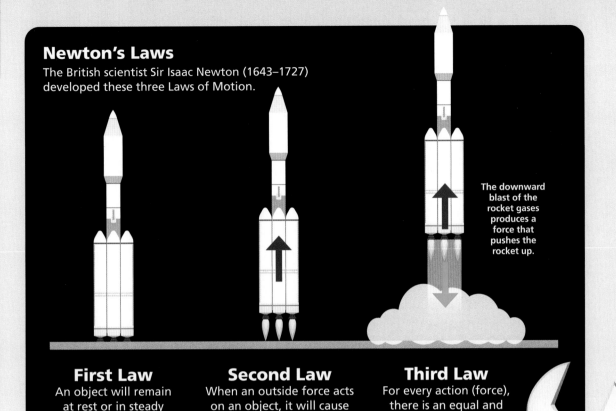

The downward blast of the rocket gases produces a force that pushes the rocket up.

First Law
An object will remain at rest or in steady movement in a straight line unless an outside force acts on it.

Second Law
When an outside force acts on an object, it will cause it to change its speed. This is called acceleration.

Third Law
For every action (force), there is an equal and opposite reaction.

Turning forces

If a force acts on an object that is attached to a pivot, the object will turn around the pivot in the direction of the force. This turning force is called a moment. The moment is measured by multiplying the size of the force by the distance it is from the pivot. A force acting a long way from a pivot will have a greater moment than the same force acting close to the pivot. A spanner increases the distance of the force from the pivot (the nut turning around the bolt). In this way, it increases the size of the turning force.

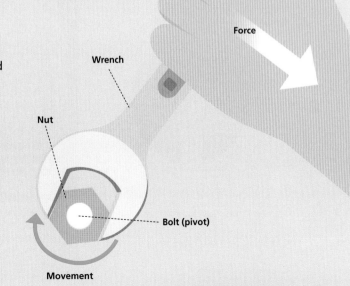

Force

Wrench

Nut

Bolt (pivot)

Movement

GRAVITY

Gravity is the force that attracts objects to each other. All objects, right down to tiny atoms, produce a gravitational pull. The more mass an object has, the greater its gravitational pull.

Getting heavy

The gravitational force of Earth pulls down on the mass of your body, producing your weight. The force of gravity causes objects to fall toward the center of Earth with an acceleration of about 32 feet (9.8 m) per second per second.

The force of gravity lessens as you move away from an object.

Mount Nevado Huascarán, Peru

Arctic Ocean

The force of gravity on Earth varies depending on where you are. The place with the highest force of gravity is in the Arctic Ocean, while the place with the lowest force of gravity is at the summit of Mount Nevado Huascarán in Peru. If you dropped objects from a height of 330 feet (100 m) in both places, the object in the Arctic would hit the ground about 16 milliseconds before the object in Peru.

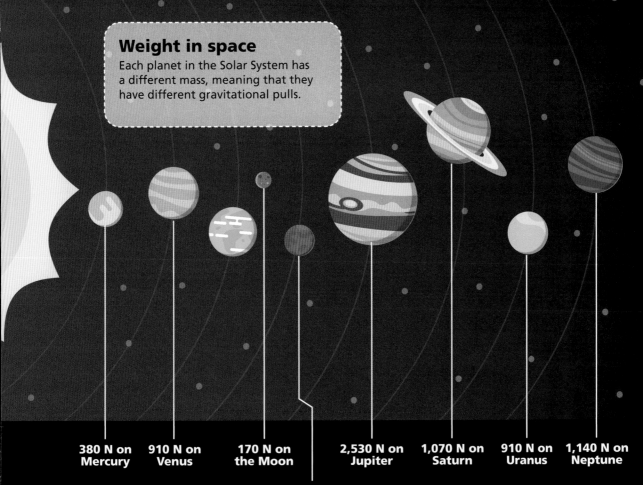

Weight in space
Each planet in the Solar System has a different mass, meaning that they have different gravitational pulls.

380 N on Mercury **910 N on Venus** **170 N on the Moon** **2,530 N on Jupiter** **1,070 N on Saturn** **910 N on Uranus** **1,140 N on Neptune**

380 N on Mars

A person who weighs 1,000 N on Earth will have the above weights elsewhere in the Solar System.

Gravity in space
The force of gravity keeps the planets in the Solar System moving in orbits around the Sun. Without the Sun's gravity, the planets would fly away in straight lines. Gravity pulls them around in an elliptical path that's shaped like a squashed circle. The planets closer to the Sun orbit quickly; otherwise they would fall into the Sun. Those farther away from the Sun travel more slowly; otherwise they would fly off into space.

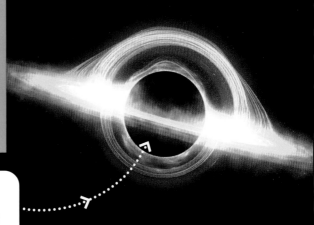

Black holes have a huge mass. Their gravitational pull is so great that nothing can escape them, not even light!

PRESSURE

When one object pushes on another, it produces pressure. If you increase the amount of the pushing force, you also increase the pressure.

To calculate the size of the pressure, divide the amount of force by the area it is acting over.

$$\text{Pressure} = \frac{\text{Force}}{\text{Area}}$$

A force acting over a large area will produce less pressure than the same force acting over a small area.

Changing pressure

Soccer players have studs on the soles of their cleats to improve their grip. The studs act over a small area. This increases the pressure and the studs sink into the ground to stop the shoes from slipping. Skiers fit long skis to their feet. These have a large area, so they reduce the pressure, so that the skiers don't sink into the snow.

Small area = More pressure

Large area = Less pressure

Air pressure

You may not notice it, but the weight of Earth's atmosphere pushes down on you, producing atmospheric pressure. This pressure decreases as you gain altitude because there is less of the atmosphere above you to push down.

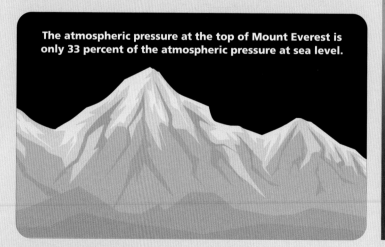

The atmospheric pressure at the top of Mount Everest is only 33 percent of the atmospheric pressure at sea level.

Deep pressure

As you sink down into the oceans, the water above you pushes down on you. The pressure increases the deeper you dive. Animals living in the deepest oceans have to cope with pressure that is hundreds of times greater than the pressure at the surface.

FRICTION

When two objects rub against each other, they produce a force called friction. This force acts against the direction of movement. Friction makes it harder for objects to move or, if it is great enough, can stop all movement completely.

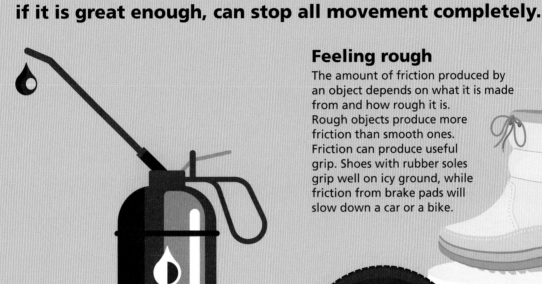

Feeling rough

The amount of friction produced by an object depends on what it is made from and how rough it is. Rough objects produce more friction than smooth ones. Friction can produce useful grip. Shoes with rubber soles grip well on icy ground, while friction from brake pads will slow down a car or a bike.

Smoothing things out

Friction often causes problems as it can take a lot of energy to overcome its force. To reduce friction it is helpful to use a lubricant, such as oil or water. The lubricant sits between the surfaces of two objects reducing the friction between them.

Air resistance

The air around you is made up of lots of tiny particles. Moving past these particles produces a frictional force called air resistance, or drag. Vehicle designers develop special shapes for cars, bikes, and trucks to limit the effects of drag, making it easier for them to move through air.

Have you ever wondered how a large ship can float on the ocean's surface, but a small stone will sink to the bottom? The reason for this is the size of a force called upthrust.

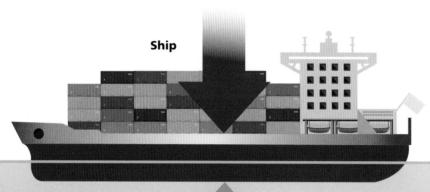

Ship

Balancing act

When an object sits in water, it pushes down with its weight and sinks into the water. In doing so it pushes aside, or displaces, a volume of water. At the same time, the weight of the displaced water pushes up on the object with an upthrust. If the upthrust is equal to the weight of the object, it will float. This is why ships float.

Weight   Upthrust

Stone

The OOCL *Hong Kong* is one of the biggest container ships ever built. It is nearly

1,312 feet long and 194 feet wide

and has a displacement (fully loaded weight) of

283,477 tons.

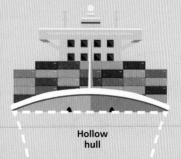

Hollow hull

Hollow hulls

The hulls of boats are hollow. This makes the boats lighter than the volume of water they displace, even if they are laden with huge cargo containers.

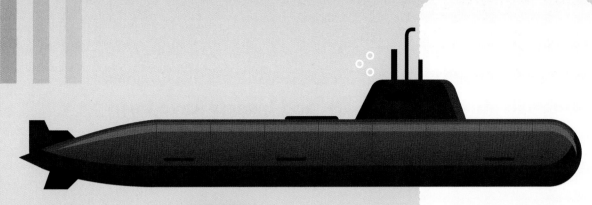

Submarines

A submarine has special tanks in its hull into which it can pump air. This makes it less dense so that it rises through the water. In order to sink, water is pumped into the tanks to make the submarine more dense.

Fish

Many fish have small sacs in them called swim bladders. When the bladders fill with air, this makes the fish less dense and they rise through the water. The fish squeeze air out of the swim bladders to become more dense and sink. Some fish, such as sharks, don't have swim bladders. They use their fins to move up and down in the water.

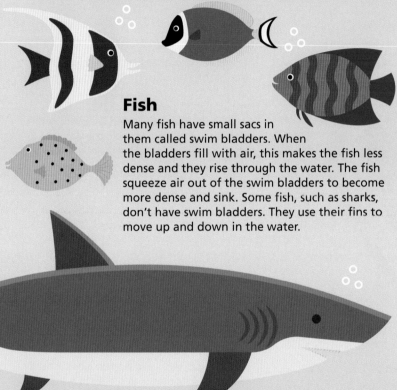

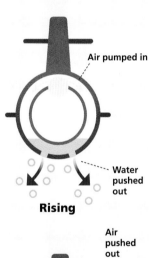

Air pumped in

Water pushed out

Rising

Air pushed out

Water in

Sinking

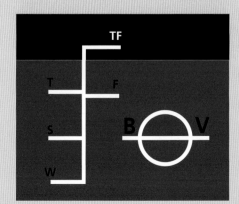

Plimsoll line

The more a ship has to carry, the lower it will sit in the water. Ocean-going ships have special marks on the side called the Plimsoll line, which show the safe load the ship can carry.

Animals such as birds, bats, and insects have been able to fly for millions of years. Humans have taken to the air in just the last few hundred years, carried along by ingenious flying machines.

Lighter than air

The earliest human flights were made using hot-air balloons. These use a burner to heat the air inside a large sac, called an envelope. As the air inside the envelope warms up, it expands and becomes less dense than the air outside the envelope. This causes the envelope to rise, pulling the balloon into the air with its passengers in a basket below.

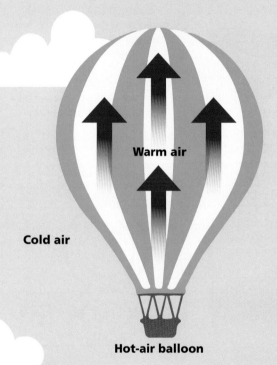

Warm air

Cold air

Hot-air balloon

The gases hydrogen and helium are much lighter than air. Filling large sacs with these gases causes them to rise. Airships were originally filled with sacs of hydrogen, but this gas was very unstable and could explode. After a series of terrible accidents, such as the loss of the *Hindenburg* in 1937, airships stopped using hydrogen. Modern airships and blimps use safer helium.

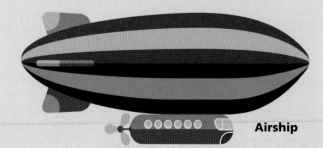

Airship

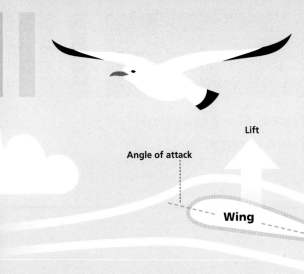

How wings work

Birds, insects, bats, and planes have one thing in common (or rather, two): wings. These horizontal extensions are tilted slightly downward from their front leading edge. The angle of this tilt is called the angle of attack. As the wings move through the air, they deflect the air down, which in turn produces an upward force on the wings, pushing them higher into the air. This upward force is called lift.

Lift

Angle of attack

Wing

Air deflected down

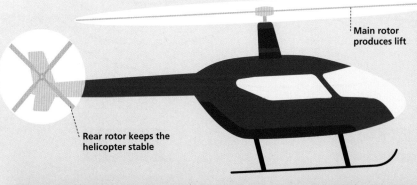

Using the air

Soaring birds and unpowered gliders rise into the air by hitching a ride on rising currents of air called thermals. These are columns of air that are warmer than the surrounding air. The thermals rise up, carrying birds and gliders with them.

Main rotor produces lift

Rotary wings

While many aircraft have fixed wings, helicopters are powered by rotary wings. They produce lift as they spin. This means that the helicopter doesn't have to move forward when it flies, and can hover.

Rear rotor keeps the helicopter stable

Wings on cars

Some fast cars have wings, but they aren't there to make them fly. The wings on these cars are upside-down. As they move through the air, they push the air up. This produces a downward force called downforce. The downforce pushes the car into the road or racetrack, improving the car's grip on the road.

Air deflected up

Downforce

Wing

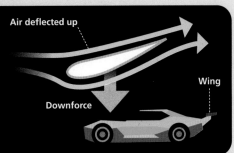

Magnetic materials produce a force that can pull objects toward them or push them away.

Magnetic fields

Magnets have two ends or poles—a north pole and a south pole. The magnetic field is the space around a magnet where it can affect magnetic materials.

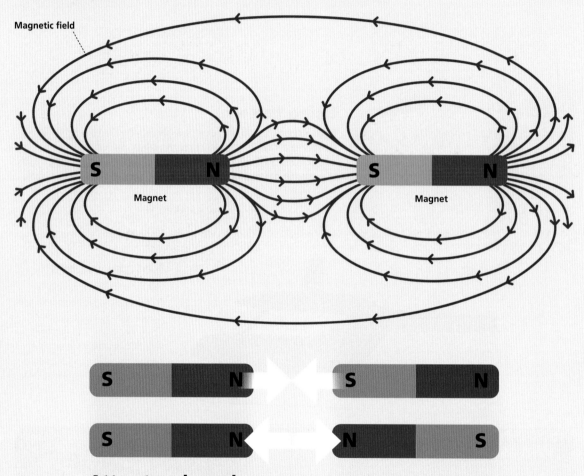

Magnetic field

Magnet

Magnet

Attract and repel

When you place two magnets close to one another, interesting things start to happen. If two opposite poles (a north pole and a south pole) are near each other, they are attracted and pull on one another. But if two similar poles are close (two south poles or two north poles), they repel each other and push one another away.

Magnetic Earth

Deep inside our planet, a core of super-hot iron is churning about. This churning motion turns Earth into an enormous magnet, producing a huge magnetic field that surrounds the entire planet.

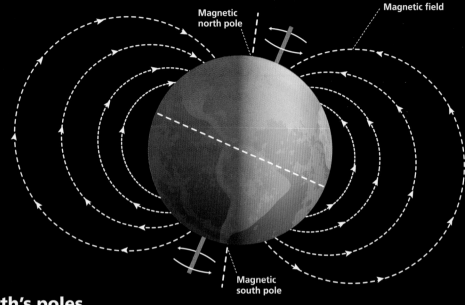

Magnetic north pole

Magnetic field

Magnetic south pole

Earth's poles

As with any magnet, Earth has two poles: a north magnetic pole and a south magnetic pole. You can detect Earth's magnetic field using a compass. The magnetized needle inside the compass will spin around and line up with Earth's magnetic field, pointing the way to the poles.

Earth's protective field

Earth's magnetic field helps protect the planet from the Sun's harmful radiation. The magnetic field deflects this radiation, but where the field dips over the poles, it is funneled down toward the surface. As it enters the atmosphere, it reacts with air particles, creating glowing lights, known as aurorae or the northern and southern lights.

Creating magnets

You can make some materials magnetic by rubbing them in one direction with a magnet. This causes the particles inside the material to line up in the same direction.

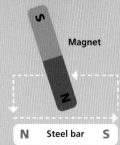

Magnet

N   Steel bar   S

An electric current has a magnetic field around it. When electricity is passed through a coil of wire, it causes a magnetic field. The field disappears when the current is turned off.

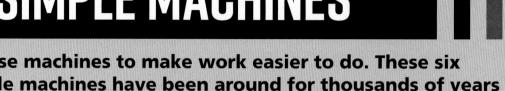

SIMPLE MACHINES

We use machines to make work easier to do. These six simple machines have been around for thousands of years and they change the size or direction of a force.

Levers

A lever is a rod or stiff object that rotates around a pivot, or fulcrum. Levers use a force, or effort, to lift a load. There are three classes of lever, depending on the positioning of the load, effort, and fulcrum.

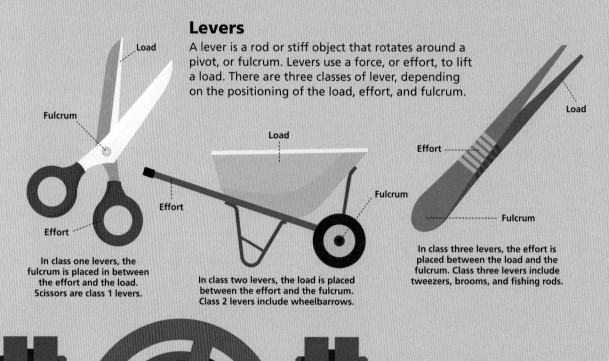

Load

Fulcrum

Effort

In class one levers, the fulcrum is placed in between the effort and the load. Scissors are class 1 levers.

Load

Effort

Fulcrum

In class two levers, the load is placed between the effort and the fulcrum. Class 2 levers include wheelbarrows.

Load

Effort

Fulcrum

In class three levers, the effort is placed between the load and the fulcrum. Class three levers include tweezers, brooms, and fishing rods.

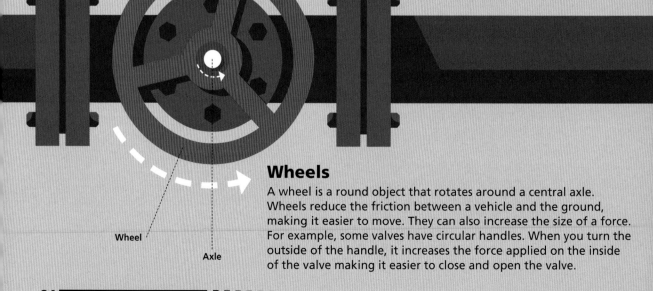

Wheels

A wheel is a round object that rotates around a central axle. Wheels reduce the friction between a vehicle and the ground, making it easier to move. They can also increase the size of a force. For example, some valves have circular handles. When you turn the outside of the handle, it increases the force applied on the inside of the valve making it easier to close and open the valve.

Wheel

Axle

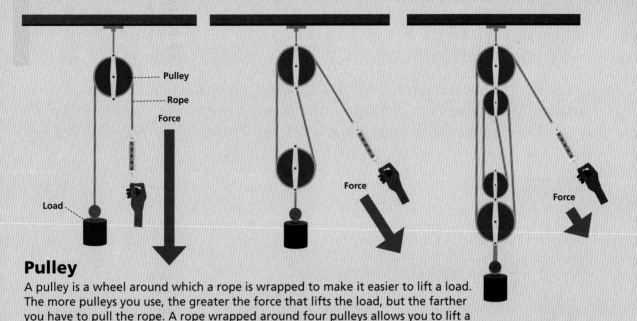

Pulley

A pulley is a wheel around which a rope is wrapped to make it easier to lift a load. The more pulleys you use, the greater the force that lifts the load, but the farther you have to pull the rope. A rope wrapped around four pulleys allows you to lift a load that is four times heavier, but you have to pull the rope four times farther.

Inclined plane

An inclined plane, or ramp, helps to raise or lower a load by reducing the angle that the load moves along. The shallower the angle of the ramp, the easier it is to push a load up it, but the longer the ramp has to be to rise the same height.

Screw

A screw is an inclined plane that is wrapped around a central core. Examples of screws include spiral staircases and wood screws.

Wedge

A wedge is a triangular machine that changes the direction of a force. When a force is applied to the flat end of the wedge, the resultant force acts at angles out from the sloping sides of the wedge. Examples of wedges include axes and pins.

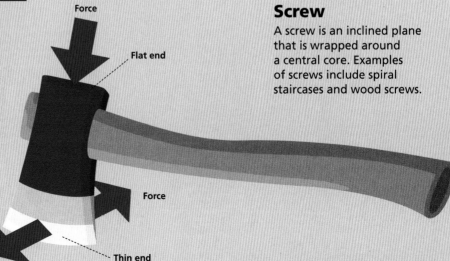

People or animals can only provide so much power to move machines or vehicles. To give a machine more power requires an engine—whether it's to carry your family along a road, or to blast a satellite into space.

Steam power

Steam engines use an external energy source, such as burning coal, to heat water so that it boils and turns into steam. This steam builds up and creates pressure, which can be used to push pistons back and forth.

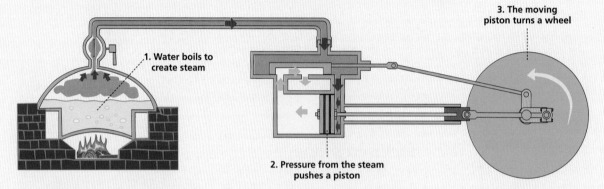

1. Water boils to create steam

2. Pressure from the steam pushes a piston

3. The moving piston turns a wheel

Internal combustion

This type of engine mixes fuel and air inside a cylinder. The mixture is squeezed and set alight. This explosion drives a piston down. As the piston rises again, it pushes out the exhaust gases, before falling and sucking in the fuel and air mixture. The process repeats itself thousands of times every second.

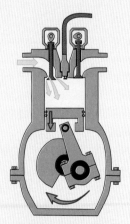
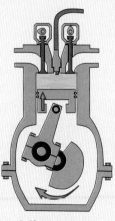
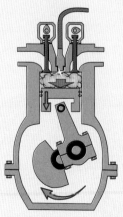

1. Piston moves down, taking in fuel and air

2. Piston moves up, compressing the mixture

3. Fuel ignites, pushing piston down

4. Piston moves up, forcing out exhaust fumes

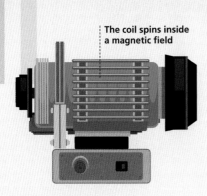

The coil spins inside a magnetic field

Electric motor

Passing an electric current through a wire coil creates a magnetic field around the coil. If the coil is free to spin and sitting inside a magnetic field, the interaction of the two fields causes the coil to rotate. This is how electric motors work.

Jet engine

A jet engine draws in air using large turbines at the front. The air is squeezed inside the engine and mixed with fuel before being set alight. This produces a jet of hot gases, which shoot out of the back of the engine, pushing it and the vehicle it is attached to forward. In some aircraft, this jet of hot gases is used to turn a large propeller to produce forward force, or thrust.

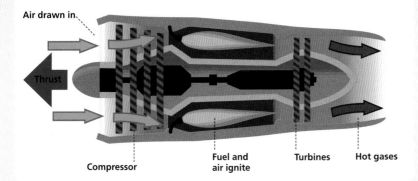

Air drawn in

Thrust

Compressor

Fuel and air ignite

Turbines

Hot gases

Rocket power

A rocket is a powerful engine that mixes a fuel and an oxidizer and sets them alight, creating a powerful blast of hot gases. The gases shoot out of a nozzle, pushing the rocket forward. The fuel and oxidizer can be stored inside the rocket in liquid form or as a mixture of solid granules.

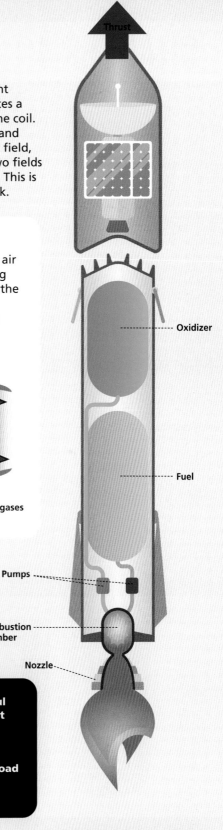

Thrust

Oxidizer

Fuel

Pumps

Combustion chamber

Nozzle

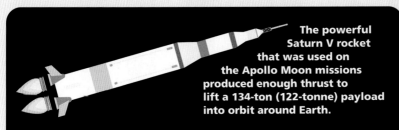

The powerful Saturn V rocket that was used on the Apollo Moon missions produced enough thrust to lift a 134-ton (122-tonne) payload into orbit around Earth.

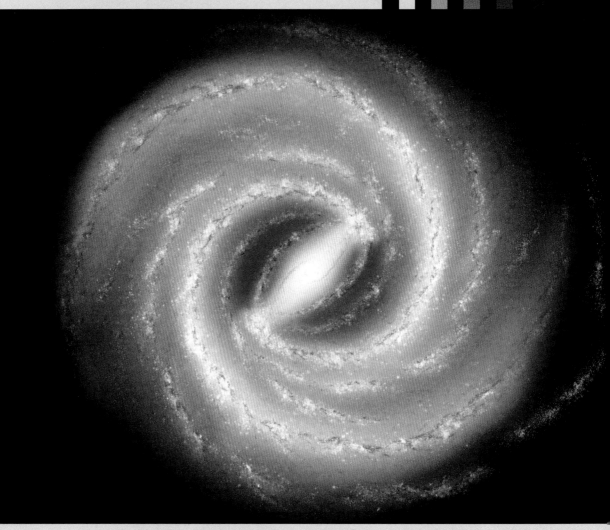

CHAPTER 4

SPACE

EXPLORING SPACE

Scientists who study space are called astronomers. They investigate objects far beyond Earth using telescopes or by collecting data from probes sent into space.

Looking into space

Telescopes use lenses and mirrors to collect light from space. They produce a magnified image so that people can study things that are very far away. The first person to use a telescope to study space was the Italian scientist Galileo Galilei. In 1609, he used a telescope to study features of the Moon. He later discovered four moons orbiting the planet Jupiter and described the rings of Saturn.

Astronomers often use invisible parts of the electromagnetic spectrum (see pages 42–43) to study objects in space. Very hot objects, such as stars and black holes, give off lots of high-energy rays, such as X-rays and gamma rays. Cooler objects, such as gas clouds, give off low-energy rays, such as radio waves.

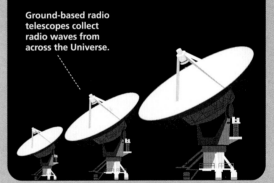

Ground-based radio telescopes collect radio waves from across the Universe.

Exploring space

Earth's atmosphere can block out parts of the electromagnetic spectrum and distort visible light rays. Space telescopes in orbit around Earth get a crystal-clear view of the Universe without this interference. We have also sent robot space probes to fly past, orbit, and even land on other bodies in our Solar System, while robotic rovers have explored the surfaces of the Moon and Mars. Some of these probes have traveled so far that they have left the Solar System altogether and are now flying through interstellar space.

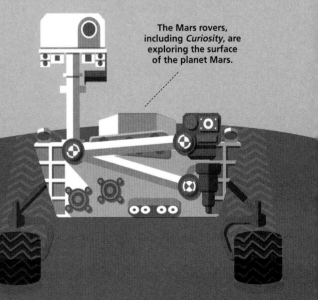

The Mars rovers, including *Curiosity*, are exploring the surface of the planet Mars.

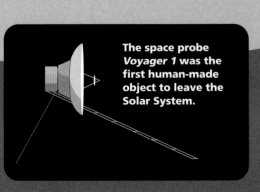

The space probe *Voyager 1* was the first human-made object to leave the Solar System.

THE SOLAR SYSTEM

A huge burning ball of hot gas sits at the center of the Solar System. Orbiting this shining star are eight planets and millions of chunks of rock and ice.

Planet types

The eight planets are divided into three types:

Rocky planets
Mercury, Venus, Earth, and Mars

Gas giants
Jupiter and Saturn

Ice giants
Uranus and Neptune

Sun

Mercury
Diameter:
3,032 miles
Distance from Sun:
36 million km
Time to orbit Sun:
88.0 days
Average temperature:
333°F

Earth
Diameter:
7,926 miles
Distance from Sun:
93 million miles
Time to orbit Sun:
365.2 days
Average temperature:
59°F

The Great Red Spot on Jupiter is a powerful storm that's bigger than Earth and has been raging for at least 350 years.

Venus
Diameter:
7,521 miles
Distance from Sun:
67.2 million miles
Time to orbit Sun:
224.7 days
Average temperature:
867°F

Mars
Diameter:
4,220 miles
Distance from Sun:
141.6 million miles
Time to orbit Sun:
687.0 days
Average temperature:
-85°F

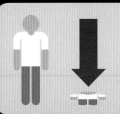

Pressure on the surface of Venus is the same as the pressure 0.6 miles (1 km) beneath the surface of Earth's oceans—enough to squash you flat!

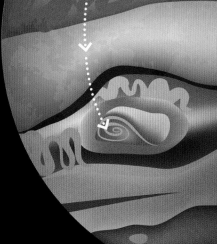

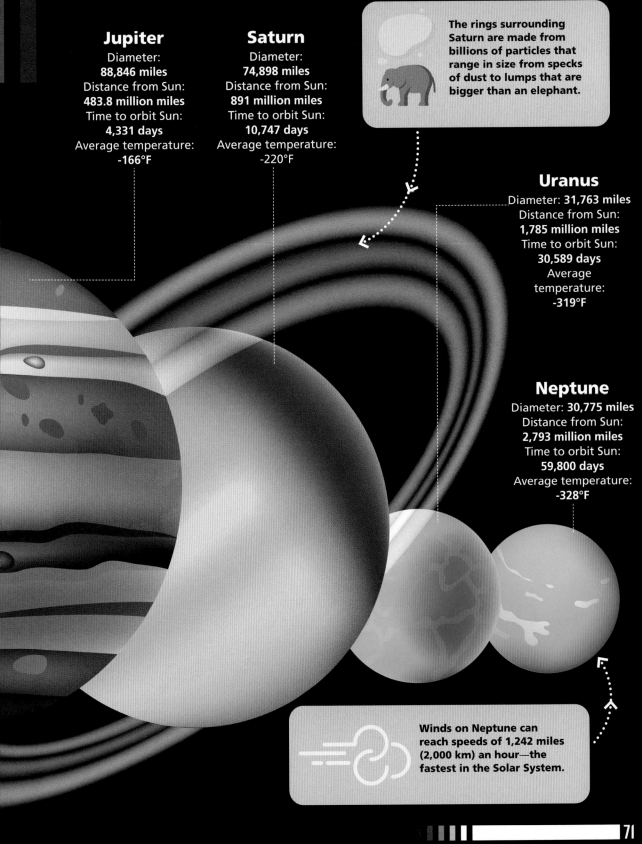

Jupiter
Diameter:
88,846 miles
Distance from Sun:
483.8 million miles
Time to orbit Sun:
4,331 days
Average temperature:
-166°F

Saturn
Diameter:
74,898 miles
Distance from Sun:
891 million miles
Time to orbit Sun:
10,747 days
Average temperature:
-220°F

The rings surrounding
Saturn are made from
billions of particles that
range in size from specks
of dust to lumps that are
bigger than an elephant.

Uranus
Diameter: **31,763 miles**
Distance from Sun:
1,785 million miles
Time to orbit Sun:
30,589 days
Average
temperature:
-319°F

Neptune
Diameter: **30,775 miles**
Distance from Sun:
2,793 million miles
Time to orbit Sun:
59,800 days
Average temperature:
-328°F

Winds on Neptune can
reach speeds of 1,242 miles
(2,000 km) an hour—the
fastest in the Solar System.

Moons are natural satellites that orbit planets. Six planets in our Solar System have moons, from Earth with our single Moon to Jupiter with nearly 80 moons.

Our Moon

The Moon looks flat and lifeless, but its surface is covered with towering highlands and large flat regions that look like seas (hence their Latin name *maria* meaning "sea"). The Moon spins on its axis in the same time it takes to orbit Earth. This means that we only ever see one side of the Moon.

Moon

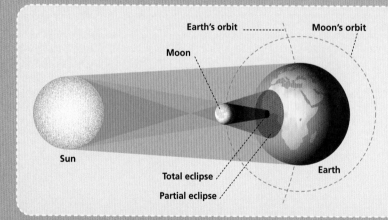

Earth's orbit
Moon's orbit
Moon
Sun
Total eclipse
Partial eclipse
Earth

Solar eclipse

By coincidence, the Moon appears in our skies to be the same size as the Sun. This means that when the Moon passes in front of the Sun, it can block out the Sun's light completely, creating a total solar eclipse (at other times it only blocks the Sun a little, producing a partial solar eclipse).

Deimos

The range of moons

Mars has two tiny lumpy moons called Phobos and Deimos. Astronomers believe these may be asteroids captured by Mars' gravity.

Jupiter's moon **Io** is a violent world with huge volcanoes that throw clouds of sulfur onto its surface.

Europa is a moon orbiting Jupiter whose surface is covered with thick ice that may cover a huge ocean beneath.

Titan is a huge moon in orbit around Saturn. It has a thick atmosphere made of nitrogen (the main gas in Earth's atmosphere).

Phobos

Orbiting Jupiter, Ganymede is the largest moon in the Solar System. At

3,273 miles

across, it is bigger than the planet Mercury.

OTHER BODIES

As well as the Sun, planets, and moons, the Solar System contains billions of other objects, ranging from minor planets to small lumps of ice that travel toward the Sun from far beyond the outermost planet.

Minor planets

These large objects aren't big enough to be classified as planets, but some of them are still hundreds of miles across. In fact, Pluto was called a planet until 2006. When other, similar objects were found, the definition of "planet" was changed and Pluto was demoted.

Pluto

Diameter: **1,479 miles**
Distance from Sun: **3.6 billion miles**
Time to orbit Sun: **90,530 days**
Average temperature: **-380°F**

Asteroids

These lumps of rock are mostly found in a band between the orbits of Mars and Jupiter known as the Asteroid Belt. Many of the asteroids are potato-shaped. The largest is called Vesta and measures 330 miles (530 km) across. The smallest asteroids are less than 33 feet (10 m) across.

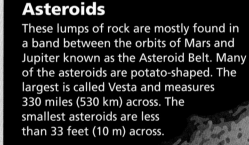

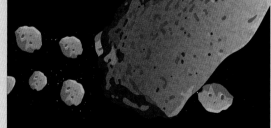

There are groups of asteroids in front of and behind Jupiter in its orbit. These asteroids are known as Trojans.

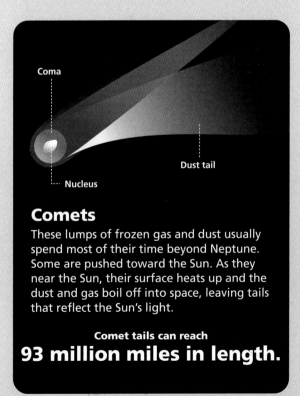

Coma

Dust tail

Nucleus

Comets

These lumps of frozen gas and dust usually spend most of their time beyond Neptune. Some are pushed toward the Sun. As they near the Sun, their surface heats up and the dust and gas boil off into space, leaving tails that reflect the Sun's light.

Comet tails can reach
93 million miles in length.

STARS

Our Sun is one of billions of stars in the Universe—and it's quite a small one at that! These glowing balls of gas come in a wide range of sizes and colors, from dim white stars to huge red supergiants that are thousands of times bigger than the Sun.

The Sun releases nearly 2 billion times the energy of the most powerful nuclear explosion—every single second!

Nuclear reactors

Deep inside stars, powerful forces squeeze atomic nuclei together in a process called nuclear fusion. This releases huge amounts of energy, which is emitted from a star's surface as heat and light.

Distances to stars are measured in light years, which is the distance light travels in a year. Our nearest star, Proxima Centauri, is 4.25 light years or 25,000,000,000,000 miles (40,208,000,000,000 km) away from us!

Different stars

Stars can be white, blue, yellow, orange, or red. They range in size from tiny neutron stars that are about 12.4–24.8 miles (20-40 km) across to huge supergiants that are 621,000,000 miles (1,000,000,000 km) across. In comparison, our Sun has a diameter of 864,000 miles (1,390,000 km). Many stars live in groups known as clusters, which can be made up of just a handful of stars to thousands.

Planetary nebula

Rigel
Blue white supergiant

Betelgeuse
Red supergiant

S Doradus
Blue variable hypergiant

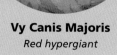

Vy Canis Majoris
Red hypergiant

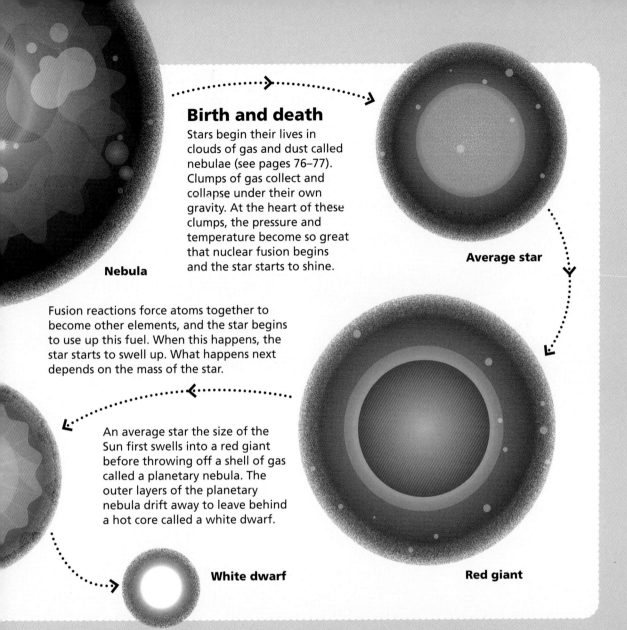

Birth and death

Stars begin their lives in clouds of gas and dust called nebulae (see pages 76–77). Clumps of gas collect and collapse under their own gravity. At the heart of these clumps, the pressure and temperature become so great that nuclear fusion begins and the star starts to shine.

Nebula

Average star

Fusion reactions force atoms together to become other elements, and the star begins to use up this fuel. When this happens, the star starts to swell up. What happens next depends on the mass of the star.

An average star the size of the Sun first swells into a red giant before throwing off a shell of gas called a planetary nebula. The outer layers of the planetary nebula drift away to leave behind a hot core called a white dwarf.

White dwarf

Red giant

Strange stars

Neutron stars are the very dense remains left behind after a large star has exploded. They can be twice the mass of the Sun, but only measure 12.4–24.8 miles (20-40 km) across.

Black holes form after the most massive stars have exploded. They are very dense and massive. The force of gravity around a black hole is so great that not even light can escape its pull.

NEBULAE

The space between stars isn't empty—parts of it contain huge clouds of gas and dust. Called nebulae, these clouds are the remains of dead stars, and also the places where new stars are born.

The word "nebula" (plural nebulae) comes from a Latin word meaning "cloud."

Star nurseries

Because they contain so much gas and dust, nebulae are sometimes the places where new stars are born (see pages 74–75).

Dark clouds

Some nebulae look like black clumps in the night sky. The dust from these nebulae blocks the light from any stars behind them.

Earth

Dark nebula

Scattered blue light

Hot Star

Glowing nebula

Glowing clouds

Certain types of nebulae look like they are glowing. Some are reflecting the light from nearby stars. These are called reflection nebulae. Others are absorbing energy from nearby stars and this makes particles in the nebulae glow. These are known as emission nebulae, because they emit light and radiation.

Star remains

Larger stars explode in a supernova, scattering their remains into space and creating a vast cloud of gas and dust. After a less-violent explosion from a smaller star, the outer layers of the star are thrown off, creating a circle of gas and dust. This is called a planetary nebula, because early astronomers mistakenly thought these circular shapes were planets.

GALAXIES

The Sun is part of a family of stars grouped together to form a galaxy, known as the Milky Way. Galaxies vary in size and shape from clumps containing a few thousand stars to enormous giants containing 1 trillion stars!

Our galaxy

The Milky Way gets its name from the milky band of stars it forms across the night sky. It looks like this because we see it edge-on. In fact, the Milky Way is a large, flat spiral that measures about 100,000 light years across.

Astronomers calculate that the Milky Way contains about 100 billion stars. They also believe that the Milky Way is only one of 10 trillion galaxies in the Universe!

Sun

Galaxy types

Galaxies are divided
into four types:

Spirals

Like the Milky Way, spiral
galaxies have a central bulge
from which large arms of stars
and nebulae spiral out. Some
spiral galaxies have a distinct
bar of stars running through
the middle. These are known
as barred spirals.

Elliptical

Elliptical galaxies are
spherical or shaped like
a squashed ball. Some
of these are the largest
and oldest galaxies in
the Universe.

Irregular

As the name suggests,
these galaxies have no
regular shape at all.

Lenticular

Lenticular galaxies have
a large central bulge,
like spiral galaxies, but
the stars surrounding this
are arranged in a disc
without any spiral arms.

Galaxies are joined together in
enormous groups called clusters.
The clusters are linked together to
form the biggest structures in the
Universe, known as superclusters,
which measure hundreds of millions
of light years across.

THE BIG BANG

Just how did the Universe begin? Based on their observations, astronomers believe that it started violently with a super-hot explosion from which everything we can detect (and things we can't detect!) was formed.

Moving apart

When looking at distant galaxies, astronomers have spotted that they are all moving away from each other. From this, they have worked out that the Universe is expanding and, if you could go back in time far enough, it was all joined together in a single place from which it exploded with incredible force billions of years ago. They call this event the Big Bang.

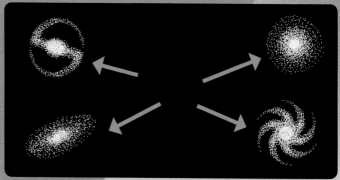

The start

The Big Bang happened about 14 billion years ago. The very first moments of the Universe were so hot that everything acted differently, including forces such as gravity, and normal science cannot really describe what was happening.

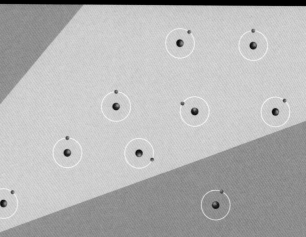

The early Universe

In its early stages, the Universe expanded very quickly, cooling as it did so. The first subatomic particles formed and these joined together to form atoms.

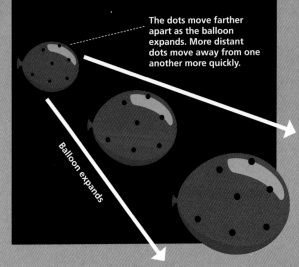

Mark a balloon with equally spaced dots using a marker. Now blow up the balloon and watch what happens. As the balloon gets bigger, the dots move farther apart. Dots that were farther apart at the start move away from one another more quickly than dots that were closer. This is what we see when we measure galaxies. The farther they are from us, the faster they are moving away.

The dots move farther apart as the balloon expands. More distant dots move away from one another more quickly.

Balloon expands

Stars and galaxies

The first stars started to shine about 400 million years after the Big Bang happened. They grouped together to form the earliest galaxies. Our own Solar System formed when the Sun began to shine about 9 billion years after the Big Bang.

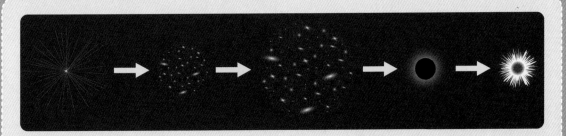

How will it end?

Astronomers have produced three theories as to how the Universe could end. It could continue to expand very quickly, tearing itself apart. Or it could continue to expand forever, eventually cooling and leaving nothing but blackness. Or its expansion could slow, then stop, and the galaxies could rush back toward each other, ending by smashing together in a Big Crunch!

CHAPTER 5

PLANET EARTH

About 71 percent of Earth's surface is covered by the seas and oceans, while just 29 percent is covered by land.

The combination of energy from the Sun, a breathable, protective atmosphere, and liquid water make Earth the only place in the Universe where we know life exists.

Land and sea

Looking from space, Earth appears to be a largely blue ball with smaller areas of brown, gray, white, and green. The blue regions are the planet's seas and oceans, while the brown, gray, white, and green regions are its land masses.

Billions of years ago, volcanic activity released gases from inside Earth, which formed the atmosphere. Water in the atmosphere may have come from passing comets.

The larger landmasses are called continents. They are North America, South America, Europe, Africa, Asia, Australia, and Antarctica.

Fiery formation

In the early days of the Solar System, the Sun was surrounded by a disc of dust and rocks. These started to clump together to form protoplanets. As these grew, their gravity attracted more rocks, which slammed into the surface to produce red-hot planets. Over time, Earth cooled and a hard crust formed on its surface.

Beneath our planet's surface, huge forces are at work, squashing and squeezing the rocks that form Earth's interior, and producing movements in the rock that change continents.

Oceanic crust

The solid crust forms the outermost layer of Earth. There are two types of crust. Oceanic crust is more dense than continental crust. The crust contains up to 100 elements, the most common being oxygen, silicon, aluminum, and iron.

Crust

Depth: **43 miles**
Temperature: **72°F**
State: **Solid**

Making waves

Scientists are able to work out the structure of the inside of Earth by studying how the powerful shock waves caused by earthquakes behave as they travel through the planet's interior.

Continental crust

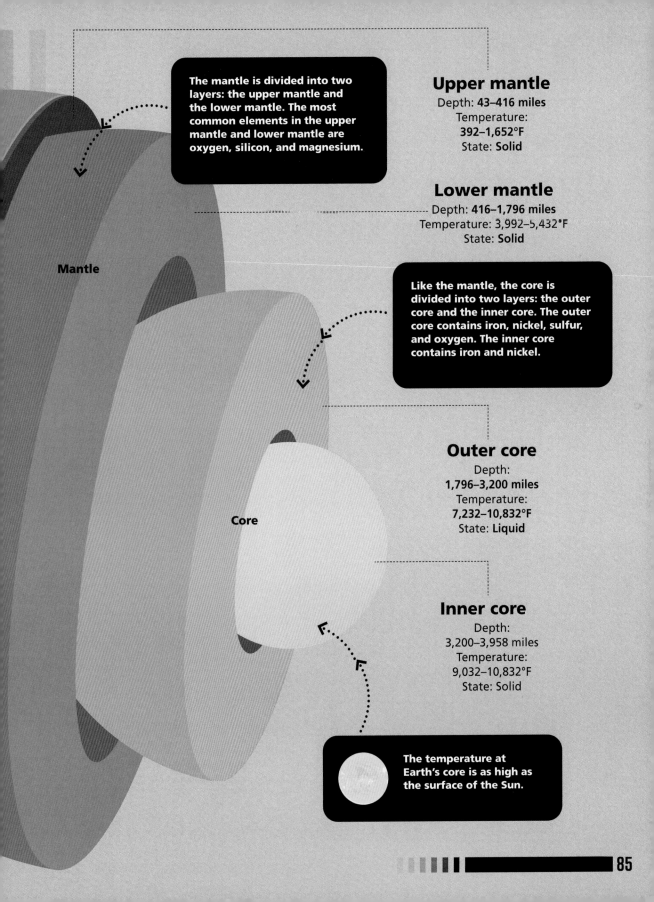

The mantle is divided into two layers: the upper mantle and the lower mantle. The most common elements in the upper mantle and lower mantle are oxygen, silicon, and magnesium.

Upper mantle
Depth: **43–416 miles**
Temperature:
392–1,652°F
State: **Solid**

Lower mantle
Depth: **416–1,796 miles**
Temperature: 3,992–5,432°F
State: **Solid**

Like the mantle, the core is divided into two layers: the outer core and the inner core. The outer core contains iron, nickel, sulfur, and oxygen. The inner core contains iron and nickel.

Mantle

Outer core
Depth:
1,796–3,200 miles
Temperature:
7,232–10,832°F
State: **Liquid**

Core

Inner core
Depth:
3,200–3,958 miles
Temperature:
9,032–10,832°F
State: Solid

The temperature at Earth's core is as high as the surface of the Sun.

The crust that makes up Earth's surface is shattered into several enormous sheets of rock, known as tectonic plates. As these plates move around, they crash into each other, grind against one another, or tear themselves apart with devastating results.

Shattered surface

Earth's crust is split up into seven large tectonic plates and eight minor ones. These plates move about at different speeds—between 0.25 inch (0.6 cm) per year and 4 inches (10 cm) per year.

> The Eurasian and North American plates are moving apart at a rate of 1.2 inches (3 cm) per year—that's the same speed as your fingernails grow.

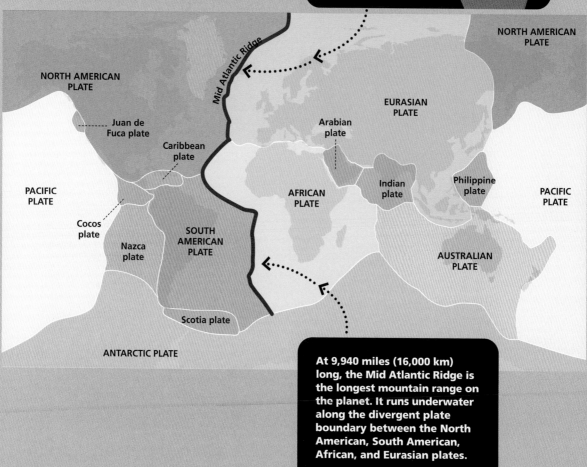

NORTH AMERICAN PLATE

Mid Atlantic Ridge

NORTH AMERICAN PLATE

EURASIAN PLATE

Juan de Fuca plate

Arabian plate

Caribbean plate

PACIFIC PLATE

Indian plate

Philippine plate

PACIFIC PLATE

Cocos plate

AFRICAN PLATE

SOUTH AMERICAN PLATE

Nazca plate

AUSTRALIAN PLATE

Scotia plate

ANTARCTIC PLATE

> At 9,940 miles (16,000 km) long, the Mid Atlantic Ridge is the longest mountain range on the planet. It runs underwater along the divergent plate boundary between the North American, South American, African, and Eurasian plates.

Where plates meet

The place that two plates meet is known as a plate boundary.

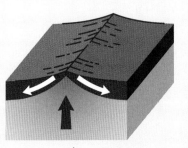 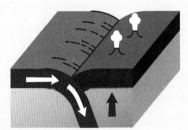 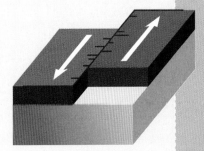

Divergent boundary

A boundary where two plates are moving apart and molten rock rises up and cools to form new crust.

Convergent boundary

A boundary where two plates crash into each other.

Conservative plate boundary, or transform fault

A boundary where two plates are rubbing against each other.

Ocean

Crust

Mantle

Earthquakes and volcanoes

The huge forces that move the tectonic plates about can trigger some violently destructive events.

At some convergent boundaries, one plate is pushed down into the mantle. The descending plate makes rocks near it melt, and the molten rock rises to the surface to form volcanoes.

At other boundaries, two plates rubbing against each other can cause earthquakes, where a sudden movement of the plates causes the ground to shake.

THE ROCK CYCLE

The rocks that make up Earth are continually changing their shape and structure as they are worn down, moved about, and altered by extreme heat and pressure. The process is very slow and can take millions of years.

Types of rock

There are three different types of rock.

Granite

Basalt

Obsidian

Igneous rocks

These are formed from molten rock, which either cools beneath the surface or erupts from a volcano. They include basalt and granite.

Conglomerate

Mudstone

Limestone

Sedimentary rocks

These are formed from tiny pieces of rock or the remains of living things that are carried by seas and rivers and dropped, or deposited, to form layers that are squashed into rock. They include limestone and sandstone.

Gneiss

Schist

Slate

Metamorphic rocks

These are rocks whose structure has been changed by heat and/or pressure. They include slate and marble.

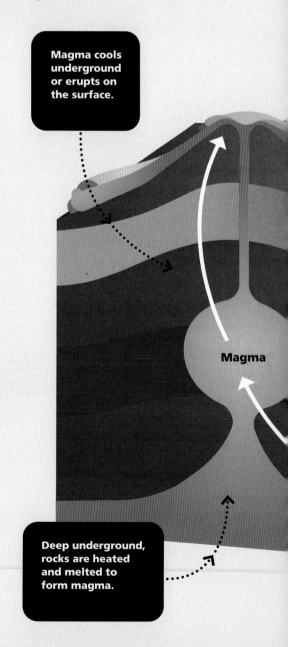

Magma cools underground or erupts on the surface.

Magma

Deep underground, rocks are heated and melted to form magma.

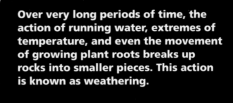 

Over very long periods of time, the action of running water, extremes of temperature, and even the movement of growing plant roots breaks up rocks into smaller pieces. This action is known as weathering.

Moving rocks around

Small pieces of rock can be carried away by streams and, if the pieces are small enough, by the wind. This process is called erosion. These pieces are then deposited elsewhere, where they can form new rock types.

Rock particles are dropped to form layers in a process called sedimentation.

IGNEOUS ROCK

Movements of Earth's crust push bits of rock up to the surface in a process called uplift.

Rock particles are squashed to form sedimentary rock.

SEDIMENTARY ROCK

METAMORPHIC ROCK

THE ATMOSPHERE

Earth is surrounded by air—a thin layer of gases that makes up the atmosphere. Traveling up from the surface, the air starts to thin out gradually, before fading away into space.

Nitrogen
78%

What's in air?
Air is a mixture of different gases.

Argon
0.9%

Carbon dioxide
0.04%

Oxygen
21%

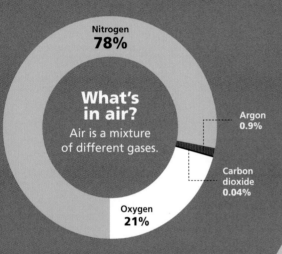

Stratosphere
Up to 31 miles
This contains the ozone layer, a band of gases that absorbs much of the Sun's harmful ultraviolet light.

Layers
Earth's atmosphere is divided into several layers.

Troposphere
0–9 miles
The lowest layer of the atmosphere is also the most dense and is where almost all of our weather takes place.

The troposphere contains about 75 percent of the atmosphere's mass and nearly all of its water vapor.

Mesosphere
Up to 53 miles
This is the layer where meteors usually burn up.

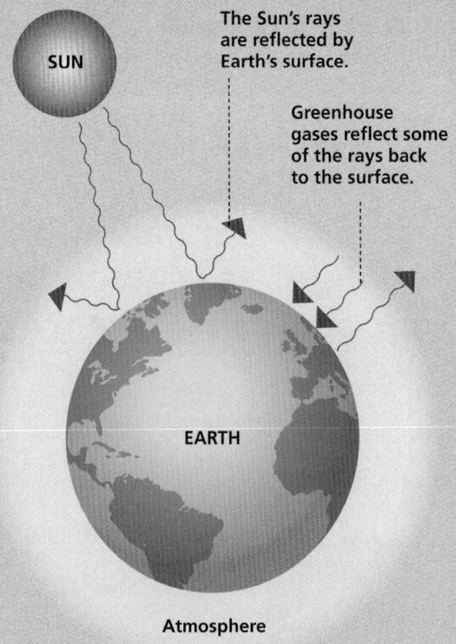

The Sun's rays are reflected by Earth's surface.

SUN

Greenhouse gases reflect some of the rays back to the surface.

EARTH

Atmosphere

Greenhouse effect
Earth's atmosphere acts like a blanket, keeping in a lot of the radiation that comes from the Sun and warming the planet. This is called the greenhouse effect. Without it, Earth would be a frozen snowball in space! However, increases in certain gases, such as carbon dioxide and methane, increase the greenhouse effect and cause temperatures to rise. This causes global warming and climate change (see pages 96–97).

SPACE

Thermosphere
Up to 373 miles
This layer contains the glowing lights of the aurorae and is where most satellites orbit.

Exosphere
Up to 6,213 miles
This is the outermost layer of the atmosphere.

THE WATER CYCLE

The water on Earth exists in the three main states of matter: solid ice, liquid water, and gassy water vapor. Water undergoes amazing changes as it moves around the planet in a process called the water cycle.

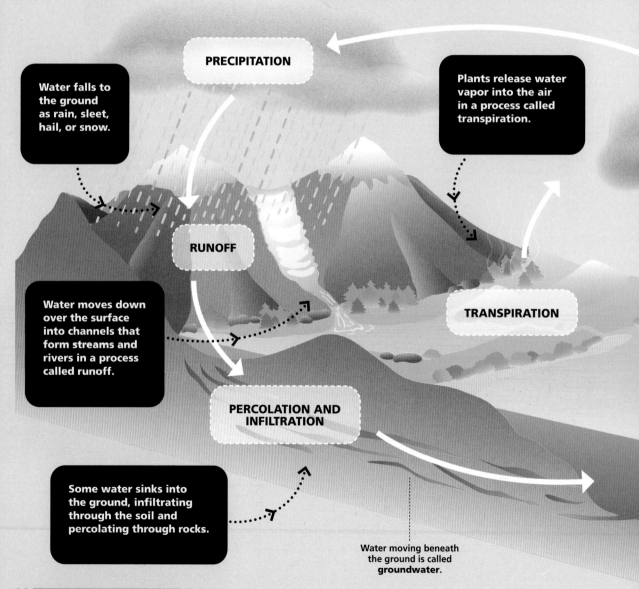

PRECIPITATION

Water falls to the ground as rain, sleet, hail, or snow.

Plants release water vapor into the air in a process called transpiration.

RUNOFF

Water moves down over the surface into channels that form streams and rivers in a process called runoff.

TRANSPIRATION

PERCOLATION AND INFILTRATION

Some water sinks into the ground, infiltrating through the soil and percolating through rocks.

Water moving beneath the ground is called **groundwater**.

NOW TRY THIS!

Put a glass or cup in the middle of large bowl and pour about an inch (2.5 cm) of water into the bottom of the bowl. Cover the top of the bowl with some plastic cling film and place a small stone in the center of the film above the top of the cup. Place the bowl in a sunny spot. Over a couple of days, watch as water evaporates from the bottom of the bowl, condenses on the plastic film, and then falls into the cup.

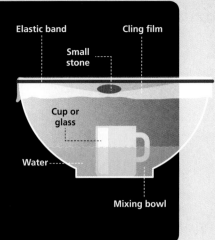

Elastic band   Cling film

Small stone

Cup or glass

Water

Mixing bowl

Water vapor in the air cools and condenses to form droplets that make up clouds.

CONDENSATION

EVAPORATION

Energy from the Sun turns water from the surface of lakes and the seas into vapor.

Ice caps, glaciers, and permanent snow
1.74%

Groundwater
1.69%

Seas and oceans
96.54%

Where?
Most of Earth's water is in the seas and oceans, with only a very small amount as freshwater, and an even smaller amount as water that we can drink.

Lakes
0.013%

Atmosphere
0.001%

Swamp water
0.0008%

Rivers
0.0002%

Biological water
0.0001%

If you took all the water in, on, and above Earth, it would form a ball measuring 860 miles across.

Weather is the mix of conditions you experience every day, whether it's rain, snow, sunshine, or wind. The climate is the kind of weather and conditions a place will experience over a longer period of time.

Heating the ground

As the Sun heats the Earth, the surface warms up and heats the air above it. However, because the Earth is a sphere, the Sun's radiation doesn't hit its surface evenly—regions at the poles receive much less energy than regions at the equator.

Sunlight heats larger area closer to the poles

Sunlight heats smaller area closer to the Equator

Climate zones

Earth has five main climate zones.

Tropical
This zone lies on either side of the Equator, where the Sun's heating power is greatest and the temperatures are the highest.

Dry
These are regions where there is little precipitation and any rainwater quickly evaporates.

EQUATOR

Temperate
These are regions with cool winters and warm summers and rainfall all year, but mainly in winter.

Continental
These are regions with very cold winters and warm or mild summers.

Polar
These are found at the regions farthest from the tropical zones, where temperatures are cold all year round.

A region's climate determines which plants and animals live there, whether it's the dry conditions of a desert or the mild, wet climate of a temperate forest.

Polar desert

Found at the very north and south of the planet, these regions have few plants, but some animals do live here and are adapted to cope with the harsh conditions.

Tundra

Found on the fringes of the polar regions, these areas have no trees and have a layer just below the surface that is permanently frozen all year round.

Taiga

Found in cooler regions or high on mountains, this region of coniferous forest lies as a band across the north of Asia, Europe, and North America.

Mixed forest

With mild conditions that usually come in four seasons, these regions have both broad-leafed trees that drop their leaves in autumn and evergreen trees.

Mountains

Mountainous regions with a variety of conditions that change with altitude.

Steppe

These temperate grasslands are usually found in the centers of the larger continents, and include the Steppes of Asia, the Pampas of South America, and the Prairies of North America.

Savanna

Grasslands found in tropical parts of the world.

Mediterranean

These regions can experience warm and cold temperatures as well as wide ranges of rainfall. Plant life is usually limited to small bushes and shrubs with some trees.

Rainforest

These regions have high levels of rainfall all year round and, while most of them are found in tropical regions, such as the Amazon basin, some are found in temperate regions, such as the rainforests of the American northwest.

Desert

Any region that has less than 250 mm of precipitation in a year. Deserts are found in hot regions, such as the Sahara, but also in cold regions such as Antarctica.

CLIMATE CHANGE

Throughout its history, Earth's global climate has changed, experiencing periods of warmth and cold. In the last 100 years, however, scientists have found that temperatures are rising very quickly, and that this is being caused by human activity.

Creating greenhouse gases

Levels of greenhouse gases, such as carbon dioxide, have increased greatly over the last 100 years. Because these gases trap more of the Sun's heat in the atmosphere, this has led to an increase in temperatures around the planet. Scientists have found evidence that this increase in greenhouse gases is due to human activity.

AGRICULTURE

FORESTRY

INDUSTRY

ELECTRICITY
SUPPLY

Effects on Earth

Global warming is having catastrophic effects around the planet. These include the melting of the planet's ice sheets and glaciers, rising sea levels, and an increase in extreme weather events.

Antarctica is losing ice at a rate of 308 billion tons a year, while Greenland is losing ice at 163 billion tons a year.

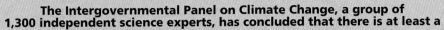

The Intergovernmental Panel on Climate Change, a group of
1,300 independent science experts, has concluded that there is at least a
95% probability that humans
are responsible for global warming.

CO₂ In the last 150 years the levels of carbon dioxide in the atmosphere have risen from 280 parts per million to 415 parts per million.

Earth's average surface temperature has risen by about 2°F (1.1°C) since the late 19th century.

WASTE AND WASTE WATER

TRANSPORT

COMMERCIAL AND RESIDENTIAL BUILDINGS

Sea levels are rising at an average of 0.13 inch (3.3 mm) every year.

CHAPTER 6

LIVING WORLD

CLASSIFYING LIFE

Scientists divide living things into different groups, depending on how they look and behave. The largest groups are known as kingdoms. The lower groups become smaller and smaller until you reach individual species.

Kingdom—*Animal*

Phylum—*Vertebrate*

Class—*Mammals*

Order—*Carnivore*

Family—*Ursidae*

Genus—*Ursus*

Species—Ursus americanus *(American black bear)*

There are five kingdoms in the living world.

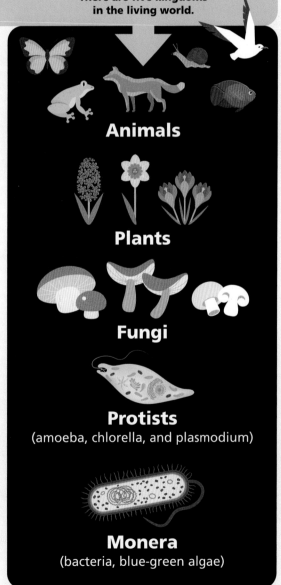

Animals

Plants

Fungi

Protists
(amoeba, chlorella, and plasmodium)

Monera
(bacteria, blue-green algae)

Cells are the basic units of all living things, from tiny single-celled bacteria to huge blue whales. Living cells contain smaller structures called organelles, which carry out different jobs within the cell.

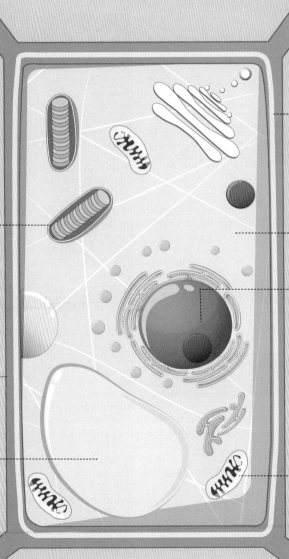

Plant cells

The cells of plants have a regular shape and usually have a tough outer wall.

Chloroplast
This contains the green substance called chlorophyll that is used in photosynthesis to produce sugars from carbon dioxide and water.

Cell wall
The tough outer wall, made from cellulose.

Vacuole
A bubble containing sap, which keeps the cell rigid.

Cell membrane
This controls what goes into and out of the cell.

Cytoplasm
A jellylike substance in which the cell's reactions take place.

The longest cells in the human body are neurons running from the base of the spine to the toes. In an adult, these cells can be over 3 feet (1 m) long.

Animal cells

Animal cells come in many different shapes depending on what job they do, from long, thin nerve cells that carry signals around a body to fat, round egg cells.

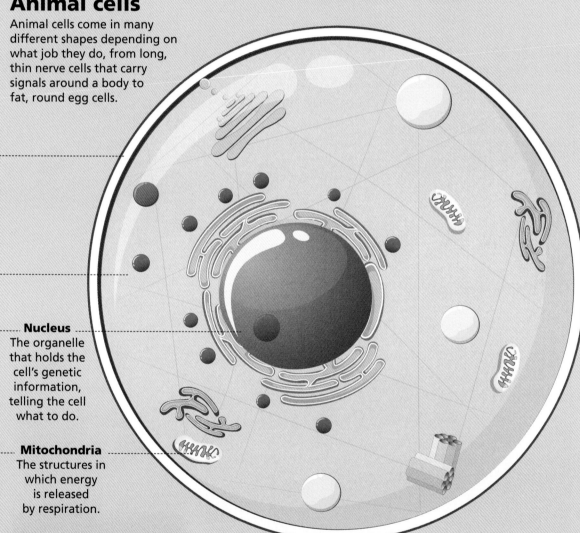

Nucleus
The organelle that holds the cell's genetic information, telling the cell what to do.

Mitochondria
The structures in which energy is released by respiration.

There are about
37 trillion
cells in the human body.

DNA AND GENES

Inside the nucleus of every living cell is a set of chemical instructions that tells the cell how to grow and how to behave. These instructions are contained in a complicated chemical called deoxyribonucleic acid, or DNA.

The double helix

DNA is shaped like a ladder, with two long strands twisted around each other in a double helix. The long strands are linked by shorter strands made from pairs of four chemicals (adenine, guanine, cytosine, or thymine). The order of these chemicals forms the instructions, or genes.

 Adenine

 Cytosine

 Thymine

Guanine

Genes and heredity

The genes tell each cell how to look and behave. This also affects how a whole organism will look. The genes are passed on from one generation to the next by heredity. This means that you inherit features from your parents, such as your hair or eye color.

NOW TRY THIS!

Make a chart of your physical features and compare them with your parents' features. Can you tell which features you have inherited from which parent?

If you stretched out the coiled DNA in a single human cell it would stretch for about

6.5 feet.

Cells with a similar structure join together to form tissues, which carry out a certain job within an organism. These tissues can join together to form organs, which in turn join together to form systems.

Types of tissue

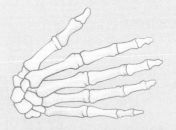

Muscle tissue A tissue that can contract (get shorter) allowing animals to move their limbs.

Bone tissue A hard tissue that supports animal bodies.

Vascular tissue This forms tubes to carry water and food around plants.

Organs

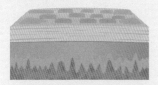

Skin The largest organ in the human body, the skin contains skin cells, sweat glands, and hairs.

Brain Located inside the heads of animals, the brain is made of nerve cells and other tissues. It receives messages from around the body and tells the body how to react.

Leaf The part on a plant where photosynthesis usually takes place (see page 105), and where gases are absorbed from and released into the air.

NOW TRY THIS!

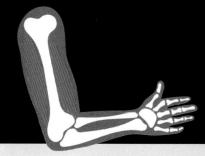

Muscles usually work in pairs, with one group of muscles pulling the opposite way to another group. You can clearly see this on your upper arm, where the muscles at the front of the arm (the biceps) contract to bend the arm, while the muscles on the back of the arm (the triceps) contract to straighten it again. Can you find other pairs of muscles that work together to move your body in different ways?

BODY SYSTEMS

The cells, tissues, and organs that are found in all animals, including humans, join together to form systems, whose role it is to keep the animal alive and healthy.

Nervous system

Tiny nerve cells run from all over your body, collecting signals from every body part as well as the outside world, and carrying them to the brain. They then send commands to other body parts such as muscles and hormone glands, telling them how to react and behave.

Respiratory system

Two sacs inside your chest, called the lungs, expand to pull air in from outside so that your body can absorb oxygen, and then contract to push carbon dioxide out of the body.

Muscles

Many of the muscles are attached to your skeleton and they contract to move you around from place to place. There are also muscles in your guts, which push food along, and in some of your blood vessels to constrict them and push blood to body parts that need it the most.

Circulatory system

Your heart is a muscle at the center of a network of tubes, called blood vessels, which carry blood to and from your body's cells. The blood delivers oxygen and nutrients. It also takes away carbon dioxide and other waste products so that they can be expelled from the body.

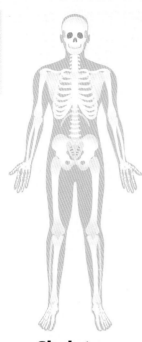

Digestive system

This long tube runs from the mouth to the anus. Its job is to break up food into pieces that are small enough for your body to absorb and use. It then gets rid of some unwanted bits in your poop.

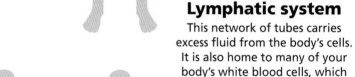

Skeleton

Formed from more than 200 bones, this system supports your body and helps you to move about. The skeleton also protects some of your most important body parts, such as your brain, which is housed inside the bones of your skull.

Lymphatic system

This network of tubes carries excess fluid from the body's cells. It is also home to many of your body's white blood cells, which play a key role in fighting against infections and diseases.

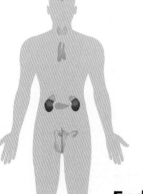

Reproductive system

Humans make new humans through sexual reproduction, which involves the fusing of a cell from a male (sperm) and a cell from a female (egg). The male reproductive organs include the penis and testes, while the female reproductive organs include the uterus and the ovaries.

Endocrine system

This collection of organs and glands releases chemicals called hormones. These messenger chemicals control many important jobs within the body, such as regulating sugar levels in the blood (insulin), how your body reacts to a shock (adrenaline), and even how well you sleep (melatonin).

FOOD WEBS

Organisms live together in networks known as ecosystems. In each ecosystem, organisms exist at different levels in food webs. Within each food web, organisms such as plants produce food, while animals eat other organisms.

Passing on energy

Each organism in a food web passes on energy in the form of food to the next organism. Some energy is lost or used before it can be passed on to the next level. As a result, there are fewer organisms the further up the web you go.

Consumer (Fox)

Consumer (Rabbit)

Producer (Grass/clover)

Consumers

Plants are eaten, or consumed, by herbivores (plant-eating animals). In a food web, these are known as primary consumers. They may be eaten by carnivores (meat-eating animals), which are known as secondary consumers. These may be eaten by other carnivores, which are known as tertiary consumers.

Primary consumer (Deer)

Producers

Plants are known as producers because they produce their energy from sunlight and water. They form the starting point of a food web. Producers may be grasses in a field or tiny phytoplankton in seas or lakes.

Photosynthesis

Plants use a process called photosynthesis to make their food. They use the energy from sunlight to combine water they have absorbed through their roots with carbon dioxide from the air. This produces glucose (a sugar) and releases oxygen into the air.

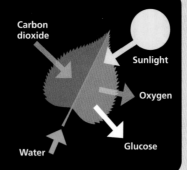

Carbon dioxide

Sunlight

Oxygen

Water

Glucose

Respiration

All living things release the energy stored inside food, such as glucose, in a process called respiration. This is a chemical reaction that combines the glucose with oxygen from the air, releasing the energy and producing water and carbon dioxide.

Tertiary consumer (Wolf)

Tertiary consumer (Lion)

NOW TRY THIS!

See if you can create your own food web using plants and animals from a single ecosystem. Don't forget to use organisms from every part of the web, from producers to recyclers.

Secondary consumer (Fox)

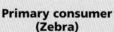

Primary consumer (Zebra)

Recyclers

Eventually every living thing dies. When this happens, some organisms feed on the body. This recycles any nutrients in the dead body, returning them to the ground, where they are used once more by producers.

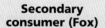

Primary consumer (Rabbit)

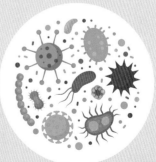

Organisms that are too small to see with the naked eye are called microorganisms. They include bacteria and a range of other organisms, including algae, some fungi, and viruses. Many of them are harmless, while others help to keep us healthy, but some can cause diseases.

Bacteria

These are made from a single cell. They come in a variety of shapes, including rods, balls, and spirals.

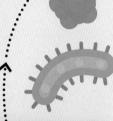

Viruses

Viruses are much smaller than bacteria. Many scientists do not consider them to be "alive" because they can only reproduce when they are inside a living cell.

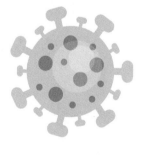

Your body is home to trillions of tiny bacteria, many of which play a key role in digesting the food you eat. In fact, your body is likely to contain more bacteria than human cells!

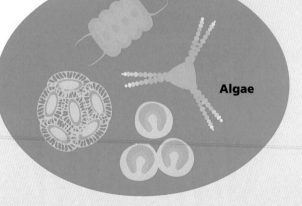

Algae

Algae

These make their own food using photosynthesis, like plants. They can be found living in water, such as lakes, as well as in soil and rotting vegetation.

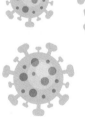

FUNGI

This kingdom of organisms includes mushrooms, molds, and yeasts. They break down dead organisms and release their nutrients back into the food web.

Fungal spores can travel right around the world, carried by the winds high in the atmosphere.

Mushrooms and toadstools are fruiting bodies made by some fungi to release spores into the air.

Spores

Fungi reproduction

Fungi reproduce by producing special cells called spores. The tiny spores are carried away by the wind, water, or small animals. Fungi like to grow in damp places, so if a spore lands somewhere moist, it can grow to form a new fungus.

Toadstool

Hyphae

Mycelium

Fungi feeding

Some fungi feed on dead organisms, while others are parasites that feed on living organisms. In both cases, they produce special chemicals called enzymes to break down the bodies of the organisms they are feeding on into nutrients that the fungi can absorb.

Mass of strands

Scientists once classed fungi as plants, even though they lack the basic structures of plants, such as leaves, stalks, and roots. In fact, they are usually made up from a mass of thin strands, called hyphae.

Plants range from tiny lichens and mosses to enormous towering trees. These organisms play a key role on our planet, producing much of the oxygen that animals need to stay alive.

The range of plants

Lichens and mosses are simple plants. They do not have tubes inside them to carry food and water, so they are known as non-vascular plants. They also do not have roots or leaves.

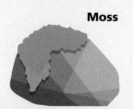

Moss

Ferns are vascular plants (they have tubes inside them to carry food and water). They have leaves and roots, but they do not produce flowers.

Fern

Flowering plants

Flowering plants produce flowers, usually to attract insects and small animals. These animals carry the plants' pollen from one plant to another so that they can reproduce and make more plants.

Trees have thick trunks that are surrounded by an outer layer of bark. Branches grow from the trunk and these divide over and over again. The branches are usually covered with leaves.

Making more plants

Plants can reproduce sexually, using pollen from one flower and an egg from another in a process called pollination. This produces a seed. Once released from the parent plant, the seed grows to form a new plant.

Dandelion seed

Plants can also reproduce asexually, making copies of themselves without having to join pollen and eggs. They do this by producing bulbs, like daffodils, tubers, like potatoes, or runners, like strawberries.

Daffodil bulbs

Seed dispersal

Parent plants need to spread seeds as far as possible so that new plants won't compete with the parent for light and water. Plants have evolved a number of ways to disperse their seeds. Some fling them out of pods, while others make seeds with sticky surfaces or hooks to attach to a passing animal's fur and get carried away. Other seeds are found inside fruits, which are eaten by animals. The animals later poop out the seeds far from the parent plant.

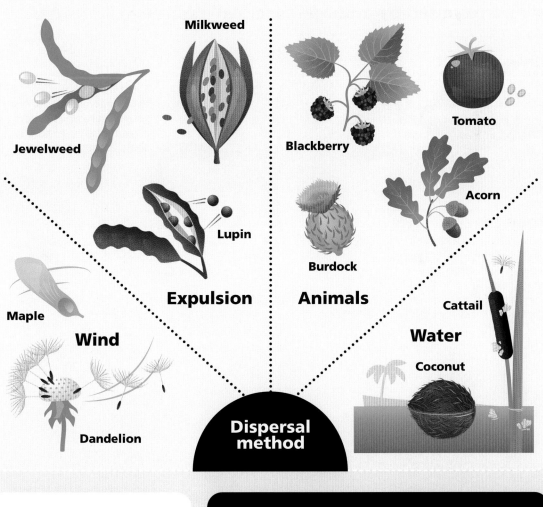

Milkweed

Jewelweed

Blackberry

Tomato

Lupin

Acorn

Burdock

Cattail

Expulsion

Animals

Maple

Wind

Water

Coconut

Dandelion

Dispersal method

A single bee can visit up to 5,000 flowers in just one day.

The seeds of a palm that grows in the Seychelles, in the Indian Ocean, are the largest in the world. Known as the double coconut or coco-de-mer, these seeds are bigger than a football and weigh up to 55 pounds (25 kg).

INVERTEBRATES

Invertebrates are animals that do not have a backbone. Some, such as jellyfish and worms, have soft bodies. Others, such as insects, spiders, and crabs, have bodies that are surrounded by a tough case, called an exoskeleton.

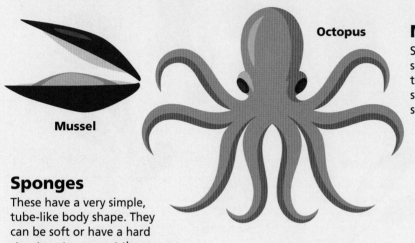

Octopus

Mussel

Molluscs
Some molluscs, such as snails and mussels, have a tough shell, while others, such as octopuses and squid, have soft bodies.

Sponges
These have a very simple, tube-like body shape. They can be soft or have a hard structure to support them. They feed by filtering nutrients from the water they live in.

Cnidarians
These include jellyfish, anemones, and coral. They have special stinging cells that inject a venom when they are triggered.

Jellyfish

1.25 million
species of invertebrates have been named so far, but there may be as many as
30 million species
waiting to be discovered!

Arachnids

These include spiders and scorpions. They have eight jointed legs and sharp mouthparts to catch prey.

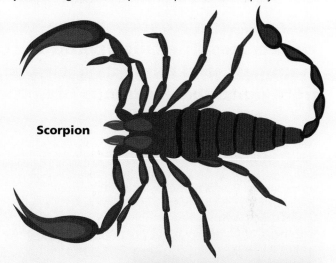

Scorpion

Starfish

Echinoderms

These include sea urchins and starfish. Some of them are able to re-grow parts of their bodies if they are damaged.

Worms

Worms have soft, long bodies. They include flatworms, roundworms, and segmented worms, such as earthworms.

Invertebrates make up about
97 percent
of all animal species on the planet.

Crustaceans

These creatures have hard exoskeletons and usually live in water. They include crabs, lobsters, shrimp, and barnacles.

Crab

Centipedes and millipedes

These animals have long bodies that are covered with an exoskeleton and divided into small segments. Centipedes have one pair of legs on each segment, while millipedes have two pairs of legs per segment.

Bee

Insects

Insects have an exoskeleton and six jointed legs. They form the largest, most diverse group of invertebrates, and include bees, butterflies, and beetles.

Animals with a backbone are known as vertebrates. They include birds, reptiles, and mammals, and range in size from a tiny frog right up to the enormous blue whale.

Fish

These vertebrates have gills, which they use to take oxygen out of the water in which they live. Some, such as sharks, have a skeleton made from bendy cartilage, while most have a bony skeleton. Fish are cold-blooded, meaning that they do not maintain a constant body temperature.

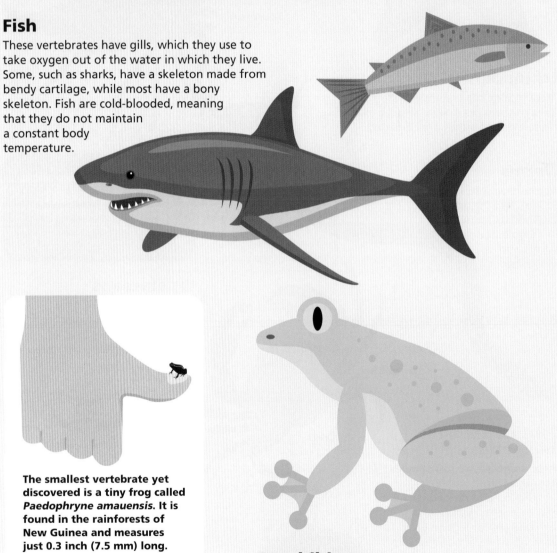

The smallest vertebrate yet discovered is a tiny frog called *Paedophryne amauensis*. It is found in the rainforests of New Guinea and measures just 0.3 inch (7.5 mm) long.

Amphibians

These animals can survive on both land and in the water, but usually lay their eggs in water. Like fish, they are cold-blooded.

Reptiles

These vertebrates are covered in scales. Most lay eggs covered in tough shells, while some give birth to live young. They are cold-blooded.

The blue whale is a mammal that can grow to more than 100 feet (30 m) long. It is the biggest animal that has ever lived.

Birds

Birds are warm-blooded, meaning that they keep a steady body temperature. They lay eggs with hard shells and their bodies are covered with feathers. All birds have wings and most of them can fly.

Mammals

The bodies of mammals are covered with hair or fur and they produce milk which they feed to their newborn offspring. Like birds, mammals are warm-blooded.

EVOLUTION AND EXTINCTION

Life first appeared on Earth more than 3.5 billion years ago when the first microscopic bacteria evolved. Since then, life has flourished, developing and expanding to survive in every corner of our planet, existing in an incredible range of shapes and sizes.

Survival of the fittest

An organism will only be able to reproduce if it can survive in its environment. Those organisms that are better adapted to their surroundings will have a better chance of reproducing. Other less well-suited organisms are likely to disappear. This process is called natural selection, and over millions of years, it has led to the evolution of the wide range of organisms that live on our planet.

Giraffes have evolved long necks to eat leaves from tall trees.

Gene mutations

When the cells inside an organism divide, they duplicate their DNA so that each new cell has a copy. However, errors, or mutations, can occur, resulting in a slightly different version of the genes being copied. When the organism reproduces, mutated genes can be passed on. Sometimes, this gives the offspring an advantage over other organisms, making them more likely to reproduce themselves. Over time, these gene mutations drive the process of evolution.

Cactus leaves store water in their tissues

Orca

Streamlined bodies

Fins

Tails

Tuna

Convergent evolution

Sometimes, two different organisms will evolve similar features. This is called convergent evolution. For example, an orca and a tuna have evolved body shapes that make them great swimmers. They both have streamlined bodies, fins and tails to push them through the water. But orcas are mammals, while tuna are fish.

Adaptations

Living things have body shapes, body parts, and behavior that help them stay alive in the environment they live in. For example, an animal living in a cold environment may have a thick layer of fur to keep it warm, while a plant that lives in a desert will have a body shape that restricts the amount of water it loses.

Dinosaurs became extinct because they could not cope with a change in the climate.

Gone forever!

Organisms that are not suited to their environment are in danger of disappearing altogether and becoming extinct. This can occur because of a sudden change in the conditions in which they live. For example, scientists believe that the dinosaurs became extinct following the impact of a large asteroid 66 million years ago. The impact threw up a huge cloud of dust that blocked out sunlight and cooled the entire planet. Extinction can also be caused by the actions of humans. For example, the dodo was a flightless bird that lived on the island of Mauritius in the Indian Ocean. When European sailors arrived in the 1600s, they hunted the birds for food until they all disappeared, and the dodo became extinct.

Breeds of domestic dogs look very different due to mutations in a small number of genes.

As climate change causes conditions around our planet to change, habitats are changing too. Many habitats are shrinking or disappearing completely. Human action is accelerating the rate of this change, threatening species that call these habitats home.

Habitat loss

The increase in global temperatures has changed weather patterns around the world, putting pressure on existing habitats. Some regions now experience prolonged periods without rain, known as droughts, while others face regular extreme storms and flooding. Melting ice caps at the poles also mean that animals in the region have less of their habitat in which to survive.

At its present rate of ice loss, the Arctic could be completely ice-free in the summer months by 2040.

Human activities

The increase in human activity in an area can put pressures on the surrounding habitats. Forests are cut down to make room for settlements and roads, while poor farming practices can turn regions into deserts. Pollution from mines, factories, and towns can also poison the land and kill wildlife.

Protected zones

To stop human activity from damaging areas and killing wildlife, some regions have been made protected parks. These include coral reefs, tropical grasslands, rainforests, and other wilderness areas. Human activity in these regions is controlled in order to preserve the habitat.

Protecting species

As well as protecting the areas in which threatened animals live, people are playing an active role in protecting and boosting animal numbers. Game wardens patrol national parks, preventing poachers from killing animals, while breeding programs in zoos produce young animals that are then re-introduced to the wild.

In the last 20 years, breeding programs in Hawaii have helped the green turtle to increase its numbers by 8 percent a year.

In the last 50 years, about 17 percent of the Amazon Rainforest has been cut down to make way for roads, towns, mines, or farms.

GLOSSARY

ADAPTATION
A feature that an organism has developed or inherited that makes it better suited to an environment.

AIR RESISTANCE
A type of friction produced by an object as it moves through the air. It acts in the opposite direction to the movement of the object.

ASTEROID
A small, rocky object that orbits the Sun. Most asteroids are found in a region called the Asteroid Belt, which lies between Mars and Jupiter.

ASTRONOMER
A scientist who studies objects in space, such as planets, stars, and galaxies.

ATMOSPHERE
The layer of gases that surrounds an object in space, such as a planet or a moon.

ATOM
The smallest amount of a substance that can be involved in chemical reactions.

BODY SYSTEM
A collection of cells, tissues, and organs that join together and perform a specific function in the body. For example, the brain, spinal cord, and nerves act together to form the nervous system, carrying signals around the body.

BOILING
When the temperature of a substance is high enough so that it transforms from a liquid into a gas.

CELL
The smallest part of a living thing that can function on its own. A cell contains smaller structures that perform specific jobs. For example, the nucleus holds the cell's genetic information, while the mitochondria produce energy using a process called respiration.

CENTRIFUGE
A device that spins substances around to separate their component parts. The more dense parts are forced to the bottom of a tube and the less dense parts are left at the top.

CHROMATOGRAPHY
A method of separating a gas or a liquid into its component parts by passing it through a system, such as a sheet of blotting paper.

CLIMATE
The general weather conditions that a region experiences over a period of time.

CLIMATE CHANGE
The change in Earth's climate, in particular the rise in average temperatures across the planet caused by increased levels of greenhouse gases, such as carbon dioxide.

COMET
A lump of ice and dust that orbits the Sun far beyond the orbit of Uranus. If a comet approaches the Sun, the ice and dust boil into space, producing long tails of gas and dust that reflect the Sun's light.

COMPOSITES
Materials that are made from two or more substances. For example, carbon fiber composite is a mixture of tiny carbon fibers held in a plastic resin.

CONDENSING
When the temperature of a gas is lowered so that its particles clump together to form a liquid.

CONDUCTOR
A material that is good at transferring heat or electricity.

CONVERGENT EVOLUTION
When two different animal species develop similar features or behaviors, such as the evolution of fins in fish and whales.

CORE
The region that lies at the very center of a planet, moon, or star.

CRUST
The outer layer of a planet or moon.

DISTILLATION
The process of separating a mixture of liquids that have different boiling points.

DNA
Short for Deoxyribonucleic Acid, this is the long chemical that is shaped like a twisted ladder and which contains the genetic information that tells a cell how to look and behave.

DOWNFORCE
A downward force produced by air flowing over an upside-down wing. This force pushes a car down into the road, increasing its grip and making it more stable.

ECLIPSE
When one object blocks the light from another, such as the Moon passing in front of the Sun.

ECOSYSTEM
The plants and animals that live together in a certain area and the relationships between them.

ELASTIC
The ability of a material to be deformed when a force is applied, but return to its original size and shape when the force is removed.

ELECTROMAGNETIC SPECTRUM
The range of electromagnetic radiation from radio waves with very long wavelengths to gamma radiation with very short wavelengths. It also includes the colors of the visible spectrum.

ELECTRON
A tiny subatomic particle that has a negative charge and orbits the nucleus of an atom.

ELEMENT
A substance that is made up of only one type of atom. Elements include oxygen, lead, and carbon.

ENERGY
The ability to do an activity or work.

EVAPORATION
When the particles at the surface of a liquid transform into a vapor without the liquid reaching its boiling point.

EVOLUTION
The gradual process, usually over a number of generations, when living things change how they look and/or behave.

EXTINCTION
When a living thing dies out, in a particular region or completely.

FORCE

A push or pull on an object that changes how that object behaves.

FOSSIL FUEL

A type of fuel that is made up of the remains of long-dead plants and animals. Fossil fuels include coal, oil, and natural gas.

FREEZING

When the temperature of a liquid decreases so much that it turns into a solid.

FRICTION

A force produced by two objects rubbing together. This forces acts in the opposite direction to the movement.

GALAXY

A very large collection of stars, planets and nebulae. A galaxy can contain hundreds of billions of stars.

GENES

The information stored within a cell that tells the cell how to behave. This information is stored within the cell's DNA and is passed on from a parent cell to its offspring when the cell divides.

GRAVITY

The force that attracts one object with mass to another object with mass. The more mass an object has, the greater its force of gravity.

GREENHOUSE GASES

The gases that cause the greenhouse effect, trapping the Sun's energy in Earth's atmosphere. Greenhouse gases include carbon dioxide and methane.

HABITAT

The natural environment in which a plant or animal lives and develops.

HYDROELECTRICITY

Electricity produced using the movement of water, such as water flowing through the pipes of a hydroelectric dam or the daily movements of the ocean tides.

IGNEOUS ROCK

A type of rock that has been formed by molten rock cooling underground or on the surface.

INSULATOR

A material that is not very good at transmitting heat and/or electricity.

INVERTEBRATE

An animal that does not have a spine.

LIFT

An upward force produced by air flowing over a wing that pushes an aircraft up into the air.

LIGHT YEAR

A unit of distance that is equivalent to the distance that light travels in one year.

MAGNETIC FIELD

A region in which a magnet can affect magnetic materials.

MANTLE

The region inside a moon or planet that lies between the core and the crust.

MELTING

When the temperature of a solid gets so high that it transforms into a liquid.

METAMORPHIC ROCK

A type of rock whose structure has been changed by extreme heat and/or pressure.

MOLECULE

The smallest amount of a chemical substance that can exist by itself.

NATURAL SELECTION

The process by which living things that are better suited to their environment are more likely to pass on their features to their offspring, while those that are less well-suited die out and become extinct.

NEUTRON

A subatomic particle that is found in an atomic nucleus and has no charge.

NUCLEAR FISSION

Splitting atomic nuclei apart and releasing huge amounts of energy.

NUCLEAR FUSION

Squeezing together atomic nuclei so that they fuse, releasing huge amounts of energy.

PHOTOSYNTHESIS

The process by which plants use chlorophyll to turn sunlight, water, and carbon dioxide into oxygen and sugars.

PLASTIC

The ability of a material to be deformed when a force is applied, and to keep its new size and shape when the force is removed.

PLATE TECTONICS

The process by which the large plates of rock that make up Earth's crust move about and interact with each other.

POLLINATION

When the male sex cells of a plant (pollen) fuse with the female sex cells (eggs) to produce a seed.

PRESSURE

A force acting over a particular area. The pressure of a force will be greater if the force is acting over a small area than if that same force was acting over a large area.

PROTON

A subatomic particle that is found in an atomic nucleus and has a positive charge.

PROTOPLANET

A planet that is just starting to form.

REACTION

When two or more chemical substances combine to produce a different chemical substance.

REFLECTION

When light rays bounce off a mirror or shiny surface, producing an image.

REFRACTION

When the path of a light ray is altered as it passes from one material and through another, such as from air and then through water.

RESPIRATION

The process by which living things use oxygen and sugars to produce carbon dioxide and water and release energy.

SEDIMENTARY ROCK

A type of rock that is produced by the dropping and squeezing together of small rock particles.

SOLUTION

A type of mixture in which one substance, the solute, has completely dissolved in a liquid, the solvent.

SUBLIMATION

The process by which a solid turns into a gas without becoming a liquid first.

VERTEBRATE

An animal that has a spine.

INDEX

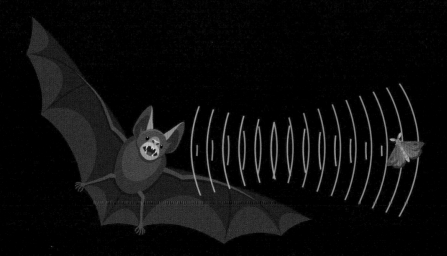